Arthur Symons

and his forgotten *Tristan and Iseult*

STUDIES IN CORNISH LANGUAGE AND CULTURE

Volume 8

STUDIES IN CORNISH LANGUAGE AND CULTURE
Volume 8

Arthur Symons and his forgotten *Tristan and Iseult*

Alan M. Kent

evertype
2021

Published by Evertype, 19A Corso Street, Dundee, DD2 1DR, Scotland. *www.evertype.com*.

First edition 2021.

Edited by Michael Everson.

A catalogue record for this book is available from the British Library.

ISBN-10 1-78201-303-2
ISBN-13 978-1-78201-303-7

ISSN 2753-1597

Typeset in Baskerville by Michael Everson.

Cover design by Michael Everson, based on an illustration by Robert Engels from Joseph Bédier's *Le roman de Tristan et Iseut*. Paris: L'Édition d'Art H. Piazza, 1949.

Contents

0
Introduction:
In Search of Tristan and Iseult

This volume argues for the recovery of Arthur Symons (1865–1945), a neglected Anglo-Cornish Poet and dramatist, and in particular, both the symbolic and decadent power of his play *Tristan and Iseult* (1917). In her comprehensive study of love stories in Western Culture, the post-structural critic Catherine Belsey (1940–2021) highlights the centrality of the various stories of the legendarium of Tristan and Iseult as being central to understanding what she terms "desire" and which we may also associate with representations of "decadence" over the centuries. It is, she argues, one of the greatest love stories ever told, as well as a classic example of a love triangle (Iseult, King Mark and Tristan, but also Iseult, Tristan and Iseult of the White Hands).[1] The Cornish scholar Henry Jenner (1848–1934) would have agreed with Belsey's assessment and long held the view that although the various Early Medieval rescinded versions of the legend, contained Cornish elements, there was at sometime in the past, a "starred form" of the narrative which originally was written "if not actually by a Cornishman, [then] a man well-acquainted with Cornwall", that it took "real and identifiable places for it" and that this "original" had been written "when French had been added to the Celtic and English which had for some time been concurrently spoken in Cornwall".[2]

As I first argued in 2000, "successive re-tellings and scholarship have placed constructions of Cornwall and Cornish identity at the centre of the text"[3] and that remains as true today as when I first wrote it over twenty years ago. Likewise, the observations of other

1   Belsey 1994:103–5, 111–13.
2   Jenner 1914:464–88.
3   Kent 2000:29.

commentators on this resolutely Cornish "past-life" remain relevant, as in the arguments of Forrester Roberts who suggests that one of the post-original versions by Béroul

> may have deliberately relocated a traditional Cornish legend into the Fowey area from a more Western location, simply to heighten the drama for the patrons. He was probably writing to entertain certain members of the powerful Cardinham family. Their estates lay beside the Fowey river, where Robert de Cardinham built the first castle at Restormel.[4]

Such a theory was exemplified in the mid-twentieth-century proto-'cultural- geographic' scholarship of Ditmus,[5] though as contributors to Grimbert's detailed casebook have shown, there are many other theories about the legendarium's origins and development,[6] which would be too numerous to discuss in a publication of this length. For reasons of brevity, the earliest tellings are best summarized in the work of twelfth-century writers such as Béroul who may well have been drawing on earlier, more "original" versions of the narrative,[7] as well as Gottfreid von Strassburg's twelfth-century German version based upon that of Thomas of Britain, written *c.* 1160 (which Béroul also used).[8]

Although fashionable engagement with Tristan narratives seem to have ended in the Early Medieval period, the narrative kept on being re-told and re-read, and in the latter end of the nineteenth century underwent considerable revival, largely thanks to the Romantic movement's gaze at Arthuriana and the poetry of writers such as A. C Swinburne (1837–1909), in his 1882 work "Tristram of Lyonesse"—a poem which almost single-handedly reignited late Victorian interest in the legend.[9] The passion contained in the poem clearly set hearts a-flutter in an era in which such emotions were not

---

4   Roberts 1998:6.

5   Ditmus 1979.

6   Grimbert 1995.

7   Fredrick 1970.

8   Hatto 1967.

9   Swinburne 1899. The title poem was first published earlier on. For criticism, see Harrison in Grimbert 1995:301–24. Art also engaged with the narrative. See, for example, Poulson 1999. See also Poulson 1995:325–56.

meant to be enacted up and in which self-discipline was key, and decadence in the form of an Celtic "love affair" was clearly off-grid. Such was the power of the love story that it, of course, had already influenced Richard Wagner (1813–1883) to develop his operatic *Tristan und Isolde* in 1865.[10] Wagner's version had a major effect on Arthur Symons, the subject of this volume.

Considerations of Tristan and Iseult then became fashionable again for the next forty years, culturally taking Britain and more specifically, Cornwall, through the highpoint of Arthurian and Tristan revival to works such as Thomas Hardy's 1923 Mummer's play *The Famous Tragedy of the Queen of Cornwall at Tintagel in Lyonesse*.[11] Crucial to the new engagement with the text in the context of Celtic Studies was the work of Joseph Loth,[12] as well as the efforts of Joseph Bédier, who in his *La Roman de Tristan*, (1902-05) endeavoured to assimilate all of the strands of various tellings into one more cohesive version of the narrative for the new century.[13] Tristana became fashionable across Europe during this period, with many writers re-examining the story and finding modern parallels, an endeavour completed most famously in James Joyce's modern fable *Finnegan's Wake* (1939);[14] a phenomenon recently re-examined by Stephanie Boland, who argues that Joyce's novel is heavily influenced by structural components drawn from Tristan and Iseult.[15]

This interest in the text perhaps as an off-shoot narrative of the wider Arthurian corpus, or its standing as the ultimate "pan-Celtic" epic even latently filtered into the Cornish language revival of the early twentieth century through works such as *Trystan hag Isolt*, partially completed in 1951 by A. S. D. Smith, and then later finished by D. H. Watkins in 1962.[16] Since this period, the legend has been an unfaltering part of Cornish and Anglo-Cornish literary endeavour, drawing on the work as one of the truly iconic Cornish "sagas" of old (in contrast to its pervasive and more dominant populist verse-

---

10   See Kerman 1995, pp. 35–76. Undoubtedly, it was Wagner's opera that put the narrative back into European literary consciousness.

11   Hardy 1923. For context, see Phelps 1975; Hardie 1992.

12   Loth 1892. *Cf.* Muret 1903.

13   Bédier 1902–05. A translation was completed by Belloc and Rosenfield 1945.

14   Joyce 1992 [1939].

15   Boland in *James Joyce Quarterly*. 2017, 54.1–2, pp. 105–18.

16   Smith 1951; Watkins, 1962.

drama tradition), ending up being reprocessed in texts as diverse as Arthur Quiller-Couch's *Castle Dor*, which was finished off by Daphne du Maurier in 1962,[17] and in an absurdist and fun-poking, quasi-nationalist retelling by Kneehigh Theatre in 2003.[18] All of this process has been accompanied by further study into the archaeological basis of the legend and its geography.[19] Popularly too, the text has been re-imagined for young adults in Sutcliff's 1971 retelling, as well as developed for cinema in Reynolds' 2006 chivalric version of the story.[20]

In short, re-tellings of Tristan and Iseult clearly show no signs of slowing down any time soon, and returning to Belsey, her observations on its centrality in Western culture seems just as relevant today as they do back in the eleventh or twelfth century. The text reflected concerns of that era, and it continues to do so today. I myself have documented and studied most Cornish and Anglo-Cornish versions of the text, but recently discovered a new variant which, in my view, has been utterly forgotten and lost to many contemporary readers. That text was written by the Pembrokeshire-born poet, dramatist and critic Arthur Symons, who after a long gestation period, in 1917 published a dramatic version of the story which he titled *Tristan and Iseult: A Play in Four Acts*.[21] Symons was a major literary figure in his day though has, over the past century, been somewhat forgotten; his work now often viewed as out of step with contemporary literary studies. There is however, a movement to resurrect his importance, as a poet, critic and dramatist.

---

17 Quiller-Couch and du Maurier 1962. For an assessment, see Kent 2000, pp. 183–4; Bawden in Taylor 2007, pp. 192–6.

18 The show was first performed in 2003. See Kneehigh Theatre 2005. The writers of the production were Carl Grose and Anna Maria Murphy.

19 de Mandach 1979 in *Tristania*, Vol.IV, No.2. The famous "Tristan Stone" found near Castle Dor at Fowey is considered by some to have a legitimate connection to the narrative. However, other scholarship has dismissed this association. See also Patten 2020.

20 Sutcliff 1971; Reynolds (dir.) 2006.

21 Symons 1917. Arthur Brentano (1858–1944) was an American publisher and bookseller. Heinemann issued it in Britain in the same year. In a letter written in 1916 Symons was still optimistic that this text would fair well. He writes that "Brentano thinks Tristan will be a success". It is not clear if this was meant purely in terms of sales of the play or on the stage itself at some point. See Letter to John Quinn, 4 August 1916, MS., Quinn. Cited in Beckson and Monro 1989:240.

This play is of interest to us here, not only because of the Cornish content of Symons' work, but there are a number of other factors which single it out as needing more scrutiny. Foremost of these, is perhaps the fact that curiously Symons had dual Cornish parentage,[22] and so this might feasibly imbibe the text with a certain higher level of awareness than many other versions of the same period. The play has a long developmental period, running from its initial draft in 1906 to its publication in 1917. The essential theory here is that some oral transmission of cultural memory would have been experienced by Symons as he grew up in a Cornish household, as well as the pan-Celtic awareness of him hailing from Wales. However, related to this fact, is that Symons curiously decides to integrate a Cornish-inspired character into the legend in the form of Meriadoc, perhaps showing either his awareness of the traditions of Camborne (for Saint Meriadoc is associated with this location) or possible familiarity with the Cornish-language miracle play based on a character with that name, edited and translated by the Celtic scholar Whitley Stokes in 1872.[23]

Additionally, he offers a very distinctive dramatic version, allied to theatrical movements elsewhere in Europe (not least in terms of comparability to the nation-building drama of W. B. Yeats)[24] but also in terms of its synthesis of what may broadly be labelled as movements in both Modernist literary Symbolism[25] and in Literary Decadence.[26] The play also offers some innovations in terms of how Symons reprocesses and contemporizes the narrative for the modern era. Curiously however, the play seems to have dropped off literary radar for over one hundred years. This volume therefore offers a corrective: arguing that Symons' play is a worthy contender for inclusion in any Anglo-Cornish literary canon, and that the work ought to be better known, and indeed performed. Symons himself too needs reassessing through a Cornish literary-critical lens.

---

22   See Beckson 1987; Hayes 2007.
23   Stokes 1872. For background on Stokes, see Ó Cróinín 2009. For Meriadoc [Meriasek] see also Harris 1977; Grigg 2008.
24   *Cf.* Cave 1997; Dorn 1983.
25   Creasey 2014 [1899, rev. 1919]. The 1919 edition contained a further set of essays.
26   Rodensky 2006; Boyiopoulos 2015. For context see Boyiopoulos, Patterson and Sandy 2019.

As we shall see, there is a further reason for reconsidering this text. Around the time he was developing this play Symons suffered from something of a severe mental breakdown verging on madness, and it may well be possible to prove that there are some aspects of these processes of madness and mental instability which have filtered through into the text itself. This is an area of literary criticism that I am notoriously sceptical of.[27] I generally believe we need to be very careful in terms of making too neat a connection between events in a writer's life and events in a piece of literary text, with me self-consciously raising the more important aspects of what Wolff terms "the social production of art"[28] and what Cultural Materialism (or New Historicism) claims as the "ideology of the text",[29] always relating it to the social, political, economic and religious conditions of productions.[30] However, Symons' *Tristan and Iseult* may offer a curious exception to my normal critical position, which I am prepared to accept. How and why that position can be challenged will be discussed below.

---

27   Kent 2005:23–52.
28   Wolff 1993.
29   Hampton 1990.
30   Brannigan 1998.

1
Biography:
From Child Prodigy to Madness

As Munro, and Bizzotto and Evangelista detail, the British poet, dramatist, translator, editor and critic Arthur William Symons (28 February 1865–22 January 1945) was born in Milford Haven, Wales, to Cornish parents.[31] He was educated privately and spent some time in his youth travelling to France and Italy. Driven to succeed in the world of letters and literature, at the relatively young age of sixteen, the precocious Symons moved to London, where he joined a vibrant literary community and participated, alongside poets like William Butler Yeats, in the notorious Rhymers' Club. This was a group of poets and writers responsible for witty repartee anthologies such as *The Book of the Rhymers' Club* (1892),[32] in which Symons' poems first appeared.

Initially however, Symons found his living in contributing to magazines and working as an editor. In many respects he was something of a child prodigy. At just the age of nineteen, between 1884–1886, he edited four of Bernard Quaritch's *Shakespeare Quarto Facsimiles*,[33] and in 1888–1889 seven plays of the *"Henry Irving" Shakespeare*.[34] He became a member of the staff of the *Athenaeum* in 1891, and of the

---

31   Munro 1969; Bizzotto and Evangelista 2018.

32   For detail on the Rhymers Club, see Muddiman 1921.

33   Bernard Quaritch (1819–1899) was a German-born British bookseller and collector. Symons obtained this job through his friendship with the philologist Frederick J. Furnivall (1825–1910). He knew Furnivall through the Browning Society which he had joined at its inception in 1881 when he was sixteen. See Beckson and Munro 1989:4.

34   See, for example, William Shakespeare, *Macbeth, a tragedy, by William Shakespeare, as arranged for the stage by Henry Irving, and presented at the Lyceum Theatre, 29th December, 1888, with music by Arthur Sullivan*, London: Lyceum Theatre, 1888. Henry Irving (1838–1905) was born in Somerset but spent a considerable amount of his childhood in Cornwall. Was this connection the reason why Symons obtained the editorship? See Henry Irving in Quiller-Couch 1898:105–10.

Saturday Review in 1894, but perhaps his major editorial feat was his work with the short-lived the *Savoy* magazine (January to December 1896),[35] with which he clearly wanted to rival other such publications. The volume was set up with him being co-editor alongside Aubrey Beardsley (1872–1898) and Leonard Smithers (1861–1907), its intention being to celebrate the connections between art and literature. Noteworthy contributors included Yeats, George Bernard Shaw and Joseph Conrad.

There was clearly a dramatic influence early on in Symons' work and this may well have arisen through his editing of Shakespeare. His first volume of verse, *Days and Nights* (1889),[36] consisted of dramatic monologues. As his poetry developed, he became influenced by a close critical study of modern French writers: in particular, Charles Baudelaire (1821–1867), and Paul Verlaine (1844–1896). Symons' formal poetry (as we shall see below) mainly explores romantic love, loss, and the passage of time. Selections from four of Symons's early collections of poetry—*Silhouettes* (1892), *London Nights* (1896), *Amoris Victima* (1897), and *Images of Good and Evil* (1899)[37]— were later collected in his two-volume *Poems* (1902).[38] *London Nights* was significant for its voyeuristic and erotic portrayal of girls in Music Halls. From this, one can see how Symons reflects French tendencies both in his choice of subject-matter and the style of his poems. Several dally with eroticism and are characterized by the vividness of their description.

It is perhaps accepted that with Yeats being such a major figure in Symons' circle that almost all of the poets operating within it were influenced by his style and subject matter. There is, however, a good deal of evidence that the influence was the other way round, and that it is Symons (both as a poet and as a critic) who, in fact, had the influence on Yeats. It is harder to determine dramatic influence, because of the paucity of Symons's dramatic output. Symons tried hard

---

35 See the *Savoy* at https://archive.org/details/savoy01symo accessed 2021-07-22. The magazine was published by Leonard Charles Smithers was a London publisher associated with the Decadent movement. He was viewed by some as a pornographer. Smithers went on to publish several volumes by Symons. See below.

36 Symons 1889.

37 Symons 1892, Symons 1896, Symons 1897, Symons 1899.

38 Symons 1902.

to become a successful dramatist but he was not greeted with success. In this respect, it is perhaps Yeats who led this, since he was much more prolific and had many plays successfully mounted. Had Symons had more early success within the theatre, and not suffered his mental breakdown, he may well have blossomed into a very successful playwright.

Whilst developing his poetic career Symons contributed poems and essays to *The Yellow Book* (a British quarterly literary periodical that was published in London from 1894 to 1897), including an important piece which was later expanded into his most famous critical work, *The Symbolist Movement in Literature*.[39] This seminal work was first published in 1899 but was later updated in a new edition in 1919, which added further essays. The objective of the work was to introduce British readers to the Symbolist movement, which Symons crucially describes as "an attempt to spiritualise literature".[40] As already alluded to above, Symons already knew Yeats but the volume would become a major influence on the Irish poet's writing perhaps later encouraging Yeats' writing to become simpler and more direct. The volume would also go on to influence other major writers of the emergent Modernist movement, including T. S. Eliot and Ezra Pound. Symons also translated the work of French and Italian poets Paul Verlaine, Stéphane Mallarmé, and Gabriele D'Annunzio into English, as well as publishing the critical studies *An Introduction to the Study of Browning* (1886) and *The Romantic Movement in English Poetry* (1909).[41]

At the same time he was developing his literary career Symons also had a series of relationships and seems to have dallied with some female artists (and perhaps prostitutes too) within both musical hall and theatre. However, in May 1898 he first met his future wife, a would-be actress named Rhoda Bowser (*c.*1874–1936). He did not court her to begin with but their relationship grew gradually. On 19 January 1901 he married her, and they moved into a flat in Maida Vale in London. Rhoda later nursed Symons through his breakdown and recovery. She appears to have been a steadying force on him in the second half of his career.

---

39 Creasey 2014.
40 Creasey 2014:5–6.
41 Symons, 1886, 1909.

Earlier however, in 1892, perhaps Symons' associations with both Yeats and Shaw encouraged him to develop his first play. This was *The Minister's Call*[42] and it was produced by the Independent Theatre Society, which was founded by the radical Dutch drama critic Jacob Grein (1862–1935). It was effectively a progressive private club, formed to avoid censorship of radical drama by the Lord Chamberlain's Office. There is little knowledge as to the success of this drama and the manuscript has been lost, but it appears that it was not a runaway success, or surely in its aftermath Symons would have developed further dramatic texts. It was two decades on before he had success again with the play *The Toy Cart* (1916),[43] and tried to develop *Tristan and Iseult* (1917).[44] There were other failures too: for example, *The Harvesters*. He also translated from the Italian of Gabriele D'Annunzio, *The Dead City* (1900) and *The Child of Pleasure* (1898),[45] and from the French of Émile Verhaeren *The Dawn* (1915).[46] To *The Poems of Ernest Dowson* (1905) he prefixed an essay on the deceased poet, who for Symons was almost an English reincarnation of Paul Verlaine and to whom he was naturally attracted.[47] His one quasi-autobiographical novel, *Spiritual Adventures* emerged in 1905.[48]

Symons had been operating in literature for some twenty years, but it appears that his enthusiasm and success could not halt a mid-career descent into madness. In 1908, when aged just forty-four, Symons suffered a psychotic breakdown, and then published very little new work. The breakdown began in Bologna, Italy in September 1908 and his insanity was confirmed later that year. His *Confessions: A Study in Pathology* (1930) is a moving description of his breakdown and treatment.[49] The breakdown was devastating, and had it not occurred, Symons may well have developed his symbolist poetry

---

42 This play appears never to have been published.
43 Although performed in 1916, the play was eventually published as Symons, 1919. The play consisted of five acts and was clearly based on a text called *Mrichchhakati of Sudraka*, a Sanskrit play composed by Sudraka, dated between second century BCE and fifth century CE. The play is both a comedy and romance about overthrowing a dictator.
44 It is perhaps significant that one of the publishers Symons found for the play was based in New York.
45 Symons (tr.) 1900, (tr.) 1898.
46 Symons (tr.) 1900, (tr.) 1898.
47 Dowson 1905. Symons supplies a Memoir of Dowson for this volume.
48 Symons 2019 [1921].
49 Symons 1930. By this phase, Symons seems to have given up with British publishers.

and drama further. However, the actual period in which he was incapacitated was relatively short (he was institutionalized until April 1910), and as he recovered, he was able to at least maintain correspondence, travel and to publish material that already had been drafted.

Posthumously published papers include *The Memoirs of Arthur Symons: Life and Art in the 1890s* (1977)[50] and *Arthur Symons: Selected Letters 1880–1935* (1989), the latter of which is highly useful in understanding Symons' motivation and Cornish identity.[51] Symons died in Kent, England, aged eighty, but at the time of his death the Decadent Movement, the Symbolist Movement and Literary Modernism had long since been left behind. Perhaps it was a case of Symons simply being too precocious early on in his life, and like so many other child prodigies, suffered the consequences later in life. However, there are also other interpretations of his mental breakdown which will be discussed as we proceed.

Throughout his life Symons was unafraid to push the Decadent agenda which he has so enjoyed in the works of French writers. We know, for example, that In 1918, a year after this play *Tristan and Iseult* emerged, *Vanity Fair* magazine published one of Symons' Baudelarian-style essays (perhaps with echoes of the intoxicating Tristan love potion), titled "The Gateway to an Artificial Paradise: The Effects of Hashish and Opium Compared".[52] In the article we learn that John Addington Symonds (the Bristol-born poet and homosexual), Ernest Down and "some of Symons' ladyfriends from the ballet", all tried hashish during an afternoon tea given by Symons in his rooms at Fountain Court Chambers in London. With this in mind, we might consider the possibility that if Symons had for some time, been smoking hashish and indeed using opium, then his mental breakdown, may well have been induced by some kind of psychosis brought on by his drug use. However, as we shall see below, it may well have been more literary failures which steered him towards madness.

In his definitive 1987 biography of Symons, Karl Beckson uses much previously unpublished material in order to real new dimen-

---

50   Beckson 1977.
51   Beckson and Munro 1989.
52   See this referenced throughout Munro 1969.

sions about Symons' life and art, noting that Symons was actually a major figure not only in the Decadent and Symbolist Movements in Britain, but that he was central to the development of early Modernism.[53] Beckson spends rather less time on the focus of this volume (his 1917 play and his Anglo-Cornish poetry). but fully demonstrates the influence of his *The Symbolist Movement on Literature* (1899 and 1919), and his personal relationships with such figures as Paul Verlaine, Joseph Conrad, James Joyce and in particular, William Butler Yeats, all assuring Symons' place in literary history. All of this is of interest, but how precisely, we might ask, did Symons articulate his Cornishness?

---

53   Beckson 1987.

2

Symons' Cornishness:
Cornwall as an "Ascetic Region"

Unravelling Symons' Cornishness is not for the feint-hearted. What we gather from Beckson is that Symons' father was a Methodist minister, and as was the practice within Methodism at the time,[54] ministers moved quite often around the country. They were said to "ride" the circuits. We know from the life of Silas Kitto Hocking that often Cornish Methodist ministers were transferred to Wales because the Church recognized the similarity in terms of mining, farming and fishing, not least in a residual notion of "Celtic stock".[55] The view was that Cornish Methodist ministers operating in Wales would have some empathy with members of their congregations. Likewise, it was probably also the case that a number of Welsh Ministers also found themselves being transferred to Cornwall.

This does give us a problem however, as to how Symons' father would even have known about or be interested in the saints of Cornwall, something which was generally more attuned to the Roman Catholic faith. Beckson and Munro's edition of Symons' correspondence seems to suggest that his Cornish parents not only spent time in Milford Haven around 1845, but later moved to other locations. Between 1866 and 1873 they moved to the Channel Islands, Northumberland, St Ives (Cornwall) and Devonshire. Thereafter it appears that they remained in Devonshire until 1882 when they moved to Yeovil in Somerset.[56] On the surface, the likelihood is that Symons would not have had much personal identification with these places, and that on the face of it, he just thought about the Cornish

---

54 See Shaw 1967, 1962. Was Symons aware of the link that Shaw describes here in his 1962 text?

55 Kent 2002:57–96.

56 Beckson and Munro 1989:xviii–xix.

blood in his veins inherited from his parents. However, that seems all too convenient an answer. Did Symons' father and mother drum into him the importance of his heritage and ethnicity so that Symons' was always deeply aware of it? There seems to be some indication, and although when they returned to St Ives (when he was still young), there would perhaps have been a sense of coming home, this might also have delighted Symons later on knowing that his parents had returned there and that subsequently (in places such as Devonshire and Somerset) if not dwelling in Cornwall, they were at least in the south west of Britain.

Symons' father was the Reverend Mark Symons (1824–1898) and he mentions a little about the relationship he had with him in his fictionalized autobiography, *Spiritual Adventures*.[57] Symons senior decided to become a Wesleyan minister at the age of twenty, and in the Notes and References here I allude to some further family history.[58] We do know from Symons' account that his father entered Didsbury College, Manchester, a training seminary and that he spent some forty years in the ministry before retiring. Of him, Symons wrote: "He was quite unimaginative, cautious in his affairs... he never seemed to me to have had the same sense of life as my mother and myself... he never interested me".[59] Already here we can

---

57 Symons 1921.

58 The Symons family have some connections to Trerice, near Newquay. In December 1784, Frederick Thomas Wentworth and his mother Susanna Wentworth became the first of several generations of absentee landlords of Trerice as the Manor house and home farm were leased to tenants. The first lessee was Mark Symons, a landholder of East Newland, in September 1784. After Symons' death in 1789, the lease devolved to his son Samuel Symons until its expiration in 1805. The descendants of Mark and Samuel Symons include the noted Victorian and Edwardian artist and designer William Christian Symons, Mark Lancelot Symons (not the Reverend Mark Symons), an artist of religious and symbolic subjects, and the Arthur Symons of this article. In a letter to John Quinn, Symons explains that both his mother and father "belonged to old Cornish families" but that "there was a strain of French blood too". See Letter to John Quinn, 30 January 1914, MS., Quinn. Cited in Beckson and Monro 1989:230. Did this strain of French blood ignite Symons' interest in Tristan re-tellings but also wider French literature in general? The vast majority of Symons' letters are held as part of 'The Featherstone Collection' held at the Columbia University Library in New York. However, a number of other institutions hold some correspondence and these are noted below.

59 Symons 1921:21.

see the contrast in the two men: Symons junior was imaginative and incautious, the opposite of his father.

He seems to have had a greater affinity with his mother. She was Lydia Pascoe (1828–1896) who was the daughter of a yeoman farmer, and who married the Reverend Mark Symons in 1853. In his autobiography, Symons notes that she had "a thirst" for life: "she had the joy, she was sensitive to every aspect of the world ... I think no moment ever passed her without being seized in all the eagerness of acceptance".[60] Clearly her take on life was much more akin to Symons' own, and it is possible he inherited a good deal of this zest for life from her. We must be careful though to pursue the truth. Such a hardened view of his childhood and youth allows the editors of his letters, Beckson and Monro to reflect that...

> ...Symons' fictional autobiography, like Joyce's *Portrait of an Artist as a Young Man*, takes liberties with fact in order to dramatise the artists' plight when young (Reverend Symons, for example, took an interest in his son's literary career by reading his book on Browning and following its progress in the reviews, moreover he had read proofs of his son's first volume of verse). Yet the fundamental division that Symons perceived in his parents—seems to have been reflected in his own personality; certainly, it had a profound effect on his own development.[61]

Beckson and Monro seem to opine that some of Symons' antagonism to his father was "constructed" but this may not be the case. In later years, in a letter postmarked 27 April 1900 Symons told his future wife, Rhoda Bowser the following:

> Remember that, till nearly your age, *I* had to endure what was purgatory to me compared with your life to you—with-

---

60 Symons 1921:22. It seems Lydia Pascoe was born at Helland near Bodmin 6 November 1828, and died at Hendon Jan *c*.1896. Her father was William Pascoe (1786–1874), a yeoman from Lower Helland. Her mother was Ann Martyn (1793–1871). It was William Pascoe who allowed the first Wesleyan Chapel to be built in Lower Helland in 1813. See Maclean 1873:4, notes 1–5.

61 Beckson and Munro 1989:3.

out friends, without amusements, with a father whom I barely spoke to and a sister with whom I only argued myself frantic. There was indeed my mother, but there was nothing else, and I did not realise at the time quite all *she* meant to me. Except her I hadn't a single person with whom I could exchange an idea. And there I was in small country towns, bursting with the desire of life, with ambition, with the longing to travel, hating the fields I walked in and every human being I saw.[62]

This correspondence certainly seems to suggest that even if his comments in *Spiritual Adventures* were fictionalized there was an underbelly of truth to them. Likewise, Symons' frustrations are actually akin to many ambitious young men's frustrations. Whatever may be the truth, we at least see two threads of Cornishness contributing to Symons' character and lifestyle: the one pious and reserved; the other creative and open. For this reader, these polarities do, in fact, seem to summarize much of Cornish experience, even to the present day. Beckson (here writing independently from Monro) however, does note that Symons was very aware of his Cornishness in terms of Celtic identity. In an edition of the *Savoy* magazine from October 1896, Symons finds himself at a castle in Ireland (the location is unclear), and he observes the following:

If I lived here too long I should forget that I am a Londoner and remember that I am a Cornishman. And that would so sadly embarrass my good friends of the Celtic Renaissance. No, decidedly I have no part among those remote idealists. I must come back to London for I have perceived the insidious danger of idealism ever since I came into these ascetic regions.[63]

---

62   MS, postmarked 27 April 1900, Columbia University Library. Note that in a later letter to Stuart Merrill, Symons says that he is "Cornish on both sides". See Letter to Stuart Merrill, 26 April 1907. MS., text Guidette. Cited in Beckson and Monro 1970:185.

63   Arthur Symons, 'A Causerie: From a castle in Ireland' in *The Savoy*, 6, October, 1896:95. This matter is considered in full in Beckson in *Victorian Poetry*, Vol 28, No 3/4, Autumn–Winter, 1990:129.

In terms of our discussion here, this is a very complex statement. He appears to believe that on the whole, he conceives of himself as a Londoner (perhaps drawn from his metropolitan lifestyle), but he reconnects in Celtic landscape with his own ethnicity and then makes a link that he was well aware of the Celticity of Cornwall, and its place within the Celtic Renaissance.[64] We need to remember that at this point, Cornwall was in general, viewed sceptically by the rest of the Celtic Movement due it having no operational Celtic language, and it was as late as 1904 that Cornwall was truly accepted as a Celtic Nation thanks to the efforts of Henry Jenner.[65]

It is intriguing why he is embarrassed about this matter to his Irish counterparts who he seemingly does believe are "remote idealists", Cornwall seems to be something different to the position of Ireland, but history had routinely framed the Irish as rebellious whereas the Cornish were seen as being more placid (or had been suppressed well enough not to revolt).[66] However, it is independence and effectively post-colonial idealism that he seems most afraid of, labelling it here an "insidious danger". There is also the notion that he views the Celtic world of Ireland (and by insinuation and association, Cornwall too) as an "ascetic region". This comment has two implications. Firstly, he seems to be arguing that in such regions the typical lifestyle to be found is characterized by an abstinence from sensual pleasures (which presumably are more likely to be found in metropolitan and non-peripheral locations). Secondly, he believes that such regions (or countries?) have a sole purpose of pursuing spiritual goals only. The tone in which this is delivered clearly marks Celtic territories as being different because the "goal of the spiritual" is primary.[67] This is therefore in direct opposition to the more decadent pleasures to be found in the city, and which obviously Symons was accustomed to.

Despite his view, which may or may not be wrong, the important fact here is that within this article in the *Savoy* magazine, Symons no-

---

64   See Ellis 1974.
65   See Jenner in Williams 2004:56–69.
66   See Ellis 1988 [1985]; Hechter 1975; Kerrigan 2008.
67   Useful debate on this is found in Clunie and Maginess 2015. It also reflects some of the ways in which Symons came to be reprocessed within wider Celtic Spirituality alluded to below.

tices that it exists. At the same time, this gives us some insight into his Cornishness and awareness of self, even though he perhaps perceives of the difference between his own Celticity and that of the Irish. Beckson and Monro argued that the experience of travelling to Ireland with Yeats gave Symons a "stronger conception of himself as a Celt".[68]

---

68 Beckson and Monro 1989:59. Symons is quiet in his writings and correspondence as to whether he was supportive of literary work within the Celtic languages. His acceptance of Irishness would seem to put him in alignment with literature in Irish, but we need to note he was operating with Anglo-Irish circles only. The Cornish language must have crossed his mind given his awareness of Meriadoc but there is seemingly no overt consideration of the Cornish Revival. See Note 127 below.

3
The Minister Calls:
A Lost Play and Lost Expectations

Celticity in Cornwall often intersects with Methodism. The two are effectively yoked together, some seeing Methodism as a more direct communication with God, along the lines of the original Celtic church. Throughout his career, Symons seems keen to develop both his poetic and dramatic output, and he draw on what he knew about his Celticity (quite clearly understood in his interest in Tristan and Iseult, and in the name Meriadoc), as well as his Methodist heritage. His first play, *The Minister Calls* (1892), is now lost, but from its title, and where it is positioned in Symons' career, it would appear that the play may well have drawn on the experiences of his father as a Cornish Methodist Minister, and Symons as the son observing matters.

The play was first performed on 4 March 1892 at the Independent Theatre Society. It is hard to tell precisely what the plot of such a play might have been, but clearly the dramatic arrival of the said Minister is of key significance. Does his arrival indicate a breaking up or cessation of some decadent moment? From Symons' other concerns we might speculate that this might be a central component of the action but in reality we have no way of telling. What we do conclude is that the development of this early work was critical in helping to shape his art when it came to his later symbolist vision of *Tristan and Iseult*.

There are however, a few more clues about this text. In the *London Quarterly Review* of April 1883 Symons wrote an anonymous review of "a verified account of the life and labours of a deceased Wesleyan minister apparently by his son" which may well have helped Symons decide that such material (drawn from his own life) could be of dramatic interest.[69] Another issue which might have been at the heart

---

69 The volume was apparently called *Bone et fidelis*. See *London Quarterly Review*, April,

of the play are what Symons termed the "unevadable laws of the Connexion" which he describes in a letter of 3 April 1888. He notes how anxious a time a change was for his mother and father, explaining that "no minister may stay in one circuit longer than 3 years. Assignment to another place is done usually by invitation, and we have not yet got any invitation that we care to accept".[70] In this way, so it seemed, the Wesleyan Church would avoid any issues of complacency whilst ministers were in post, but one can clearly see the disruption of this rotation on the family. This too, might have had an impact on the content of this play and whether the central character was a Cornishman.

It seems that by September 1891 Symons was writing what would eventually become *The Minister's Call*. It is known that this was a one-act play, and at the end of a letter to Ernest Rhys, Symons confesses that he is at work on this. No further details are offered however because sadly the letter is incomplete.[71] It is certainly hard to know what kind of drama this play was, though we can later see similarities between *Tristan and Iseult* and the kind of dramas produced by Yeats. Some clues might come from Symons' own criticism and what he most valued, since surely some of this might be reflected in his own writing. In a translation of Émile Verhaeren's play *Les Aubes* (published in London as *The Downs*), Symons praised Verhaeren for his "melodrama of the spirit, in which there was poetry, but also rhetoric".[72] Maybe such criticism gives us a clue as to Symons' own dramaturgy and what he valued on stage.

1993:229–30. Symons' identity is revealed by Beckson and Monro 1989:12.

70 Letter to James Dykes Campbell, 3 April 1888, MS, BL. Cited in Beckson and Monro 1970:36–8.

71 Letter to Ernest Rhys, 9 September 1891, MS, BL. Cited in Beckson and Monro 1970:82–3. Ernest Rhys (1859–1946) was an Anglo-Welsh writer most famous for founding the Everyman series of affordable classics.

72 Cited in Beckson and Monro 1970:125. At one point, Symons is considering taking a pseudonym to assist with his dramatic career. Two names are considered: Arthur Pascoe and Mark Pascoe: the former using his mother's surname and the latter a combination of his father's first name and mother's surname. In the end both are rejected since his "father hated the stage so much". See Beckson and Monro 1970:140. This would seem standard non-conformist (but also possibly vestigial Puritanism) fear over the scandalous and sexualised nature of plays, drama and the theatre. There is a sense that Symons delights in antagonizing this position.

There are some further important insights into the drama from Symons' own papers. In a manuscript titled "Frank Harris" now held at the University of Princeton, Symons describes the genesis of the play. Frank Harris (1856–1931) was an author, journalist and editor of the *Fortnightly Review* (1837–1894). Clearly, as well as some of the elements listed above, Harris was also instrumental in setting Symons thinking. In the manuscript Symons observes the following and explains the initial collaborative process between him and George Moore:

> After I had read this story [Frank Harris's "A Modern Idyll"] it occurred to me to turn this rather revolting material into a One Act play. I mentioned the fact to Harris and [George] Moore, who urged me to try my hand in a form which was novel to me. Just then I had not the faintest idea of how one begins to write a play, how one constructs it, how one sets figures in motion, and how one contrives the final climax. Night after night I went across to Moore's rooms, showing him the fragments I had composed; which he read and commented upon. We ended up collaborating. Moore refused to have his name put beside mine on the play-bill.[73]

Certainly there is an air of naivety about the process, but also excitement in terms of trying out something new. It is unclear whether Moore decided not to be involved because he thought the drama was weak, or because he wished Symons to take credit for the piece. Writing drama seemed to be a constant pursuit by Symons even though in the end, he was not very successful at it. Between *The Minister's Call* and *Tristan and Iseult*, in March 1908 Symons was trying to develop another drama titled *The Harvesters*.[74] With an ominous tone, Symons writes to a famous actress acquaintance of his: Julia Mar-

---

73   Andrew Symons, "Frank Harris", MS., Princeton. Beckson and Monro 1970:89. The story is about the Reverend John Letgood who calls on a pretty girl of eighteen, called Mrs Hooper. It is set in Kansas City and Letgood wonders if Mrs Hooper will accept his offer to run away with him. Mrs Hooper however is already married to the local Deacon. The story's theme is really about what an earnest Christian should be and how they are in reality. In the end, it is one of Letgood's sermons that convinces her to be with him.

74   Letter to Julia Marlowe, 21 March 1908, MS Museum, NY. Beckson and Monro 1970:119.

lowe, who had taken this play with her to the United States for hopeful development there. When nothing came of it, Symons wrote to her, revealing as Beckson and Monro note, "a deep-seated anxiety"[75] that expresses his desire to be successful as a dramatist, and to bring his work to fruition:

> All my friends are waiting to see what I can do, and they are only now, on hearing that you have taken my play, beginning to believe in the possibility of my achieving something on the stage. I put in, just to show you the interest that people in America are ready to take a letter I have received from Brander Matthews. Destroy it: I don't want it back. Thomas Hardy is equally anxious about it here. The mere mention of your name has an instant effect. So if, after all, this whole structure should tumble about my ears, I should be pretty well obliterated under it.[76]

This letter is a good insight into Symons' mentality at this point. His hope is that Marlowe would persuade investors of an American production but despite the support of luminaries such as Hardy, it was not to come. In the final sentence we note how failure to mount the play would "obliterate him": a darker tone, which seems to indicate his coming madness, obviously derived from his frustration to make the kind of breakthrough that he wanted. Possibly however, the failure of mounting *The Harvesters* was part of a trilogy of events which happened to Symons during this phase, and sealed his fate. I examine this next.

It appears that shortly after the above letter Symons received word that the most important Italian actress of the era would star in his *Tristan and Iseult* in Rome.[77] This was Eleonora Giulia Amalia Duse (1858–1924), who of course, was unlikely (given she was in the latter phase of her career) to have played Iseult but in fact, the Queen of Ireland. Symons excitedly told his friend Edward Hutton on 11 April 1908 that he "could imagine the splendour of a first dramatic performance in Rome!"[78] However, the production failed to material-

---

75 Beckson and Monro 1970.
76 Beckson and Monro 1970.
77 Beckson and Monro 1970.

ize, and Symons had to wait almost another decade for his failed project to eventually emerge in print. This must have been crushing for him, given what had happened with *The Harvesters*, and it would have seemed to him that his destiny was never to have any true dramatic success, in the kind of way that Yeats was enjoying in Ireland.

Symons' mental anguish was delivered a third blow when an important article he had written on the importance of the work of Joseph Conrad was rejected by several magazines.[79] He judged the article to be one of his best, and was immensely frustrated that like his drama, this work could not be found a home. Independently these three events could be survived, but put together, they were crushing in terms of Symons' sense of self, and it is likely that his incapacity to make these three happen around the same time triggered his descent into madness, and his twenty years exile from the literary scene. By the turn of 1909, Symons was institutionalized and those around him were trying to make sense of his madness. On 11 January, his wife Rhoda confided to an American critic named James Gibbons Huneker (1857–1921) about her husband's condition:

> My poor, beloved Arthur is in a private asylum close by—I am in lodgings near him—there is no hope of recovery; and they can do absolutely nothing for him—they don't even attempt treatment—it is General Paralysis (the doctors say there is no trace of the disease which generally accounts for his malady—and Arthur always told me he never had it—he would not tell a lie...[80]

There is much in Rhoda's words which need comment upon here. It is clear that her fear was that Symons was suffering from syphilis. Thus we may reassess the trilogy of misfortunes that faced him, and perhaps link it more closely with this disease. The puzzle is, of course,

---

78   Letter to Edward Hutton, 11 April, 1908, MS Harvard. Cited in Beckson and Monro 1970.

79   Beckson and Monro 1970. Symons then began a correspondence with Joseph Conrad (1857–1924), leading to them meeting in 1910.

80   Letter by Rhoda Symons to James Gibbons Huneker, 11 January 1909, MS Dartmouth. Cited in Beckson and Monro 1989:121. Huneker hugely admired Symons and quoted from him extensively.

that the physicians seem to say there is no evidence of it, and that Symons himself says he never had it, which Rhoda appears to believe. It could be, however, that Symons was in fact, suffering from syphilis because he certainly had prior lovers and seemed to enjoy liaisons with several girls in the musical halls.[81] He may well have disguised the condition and the doctors could have done the same thing in order to protect Rhoda. However, this does give us an alternative explanation of his madness, linking him more directly to the Decadent Movement.

Certainly syphilis was rife in the period in which Symons was active, and it puts us in mind, as Thompson has shown, of Jack Clemo's father, Reggie Clemo, who returned from America with the condition, passing it on to his son, and resulting in Jack's resultant disabilities.[82] It also leaves us with the sobering knowledge that despite coming from Methodist families neither Arthur Symons nor Reggie Clemo were immune to the power of syphilis. On the other hand, one might of course argue, that knowledge of the disease and its transmission ironically informed Symons of the "tragedy" that could come with the kind of decadent love that he extolled in his retelling of *Tristan and Iseult*. Whatever the cause of Symons' fall (frustration, syphilis or a combination of the two) certainly it had the dual effect of forcing him to reduce his expectation but also paradoxically to understand further his Cornish identity.

---

81   One was named Lydia: an affair which lasted from 1893 until 1896.
82   Thompson 2016. Jack's wife, Ruth Clemo was always very guarded about this aspect of her husband's past, despite Clemo freely admitting it in his writings.

4

At the very edge of England: Travels to Cornwall

Given Symons' conceptualization of himself as Cornish (something probably engendered early on by his parents) it seems likely that Symons' frequent trips to Cornwall in his lifetime, helped to reinforce his identity and reconnect with the landscape in perhaps the same way that he saw Yeats doing in Ireland. It was in July and August 1896 that he spent core time in Ireland with Yeats, including a trip to the then remote Aran Islands, where he would most certainly have encountered the Irish language.[83] This visit was crucial in terms of his fuller awareness of his Celtic identity. Cornwall and the notion of Celtic Cornwall were however, installed from a young age though, with his father's circuit being in St Ives sometime between 1866 and 1873. Contact in the early part of his life with the territory is then (with the exception of 1893) a little more vague and unrecorded but again, Symons may well have travelled there further prior to his visit to Ireland in 1896. Some discussion over the landscape and its people may have emerged in his meeting with Thomas Hardy whom he stayed with at Max Gate at Dorchester between 4 and 7 August 1900,[84] because Hardy had already had experiences in Cornwall, and was not finished with writing about the territory poetically and dramatically.[85]

Paradoxically however, it seems that following his breakdown in 1908 and his diagnosis as "insane", Symons appears to spend more time in Cornwall. This may be because the place was deemed as

---

83 For a useful depiction of life in the west of Ireland at this time, see Synge, 2009 [1912]. See also Synge,1961 [1907]. J. M. Synge (1871–1909) was an Anglo-Irish poet, playwright and folklorist. His dramas depict Ireland in a very different way than Yeats; choosing social realism instead of mythology.

84 See Beckson and Monro 1989:xviii–xx.

85 See Phelps 1975.

having a mild climate and because it was rated highly as a place for recovery and recuperation. For example, in the Winter of 1915, Symons spent time there with Havelock Ellis. He was back there again with Ellis, between December and January of 1921, and returned once more between November and March 1922. Clearly, he was finding Cornish winters favourable. Again, in 1927 he spent the winter in Cornwall, so there was considerable time to reflect and construct poetic images of the territory.[86] In 1893 however, we know that Symons was in Cornwall and that he is actively reflecting on his time there. In a letter to Katherine Willard[87] dated 30 November, Symons says that he is staying at Carbis Water, Lelant and observes the following:

> As you see, I am down at the very edge of England, at Carbis Bay, close to St. Ives, where I lived for three years when I was a small boy. I am staying with Havelock Ellis, who has a little cottage down here. You must absolutely come down some time and see this region: there is nothing like it in Europe. It is impossible to describe, for the effect is so big, so terrifying really, that words become ridiculous, meaningless, when they put on emphasis enough to come near rendering it.[88]

This effusive description to Willard does several things at once. He is there as part of a process of recollecting his childhood, but also because this correspondence refers to the duality of Cornwall (its "country-county" paradox); here is on the very edge of England so not quite in it. Furthermore, Symons has it as a region and it is unlike anything else that he has observed in Europe. The final couple of

---

86 See Beckson and Monro 1989.

87 Katherine Willard (1866–1902) was a founder of the Women's Christian Temperance Union. In letter to her, Symons teases her about her conventionality. See Letter to Katherine Willard, 30 November 1890, MS Baldwin. Cited in Beckson and Monro, 1989:68–9.

88 See Letter to Katherine Willard, 30 November 1893, MS Baldwin. Cited in Beckson and Monro 1970:102–4. Havelock Ellis (1859–1939) was a medical physician, writer and social reformer. He had controversial views on eugenics and wrote on drug use and sexuality. Ellis later defended Symons' drug use, his habitual behaviour and company, and felt that his psychosis was temporary. Cited in Beckson and Monro 1970:270.

sentences seem to allude to the territory's epic nature and that it renders Symons speechless. At the same time of course, this epic feel of place matches precisely the kind of epic narrative that he was to engage with when it later came to writing *Tristan and Iseult*. A sense of place is garnered from the next section of the letter:

> On Monday Ellis and I started on a walking tour. We went to Penzance and then walked all around the coast, and back here again, visiting every sea-coast village and cove, by way of Land's End, Gurnard's Head, Sennen Cove, the Logan Rock, and other places locally famous. We stayed at fishermen's cottages, and had meals in little quaint country inns. And we did plenty of walking for the path was generally a mere thread between the rocks, and on the edge of the cliffs, now climbing up one hill and now sliding down another.[89]

This was an epic undertaking, since walking the entire Penwith coast-path is some achievement. The pattern of the description of the locations is not logical but this is probably not Symons' intention anyway. What comes across is the sense of simplicity (all very different than the theatres and fashionable cafes of London and Paris) and the danger of the activity; the cliff "edge" here seemingly reinforcing the peripherality discovered. Symons does not seem to very often consider the poetry of place-names and geography in his work, which one might have assumed he would have picked up on his perambulations around west Cornwall. However there is one exception and this is to be found in what Symons terms a "study in musical temperament"—a work planned as a short story but eventually integrated into his novel *Spiritual Adventures* (1905). This was a sequence titled "Christian Trevelga" where a place-name seems to be bolted onto a character.[90]

---

89 Beckson and Monro 1970. Symons spells Gurnard's Head as Gurnand's Head. This is corrected in the quotation here.

90 Letter to James Gibbons Huneker, 2 May 1902, MS Yale. For discussion, see Beckson and Munro 1989:165. Trevelga (normally spelt Trevalga) is a coastal parish in North Cornwall. The next parish west is that of Tintagel. There is no mention of Symons visiting Tintagel but a trip there by Ellis and him is a distinct possibility. Symons' mother's home village of Helland, is also not far south of Tintagel.

5

The Decadent Movement: A Celtic *Fin de Siècle*?

Unlike other imaginings of Tristan and Iseult, Symons' play is filled with allusions to and aspects of the so-called Decadent Movement.[91] Some exploration of this Movement will considerably assist us in our appreciation of the work. Although the latent Celtic background to the narrative remains, Symons' central artistic method was to imbibe the narrative with aspects of Decadence. For him, he saw the narratology of Tristan and Iseult as containing the necessary components to permit him to do this. If we see the Decadent Movement, as part of the *Fin de Siècle* (a French term, meaning 'End of the Century'),[92] then we have an interesting critical angle to apply on Symons' text. *Fin de Siècle* was a popular concept during the cultural and literary transition from the nineteenth to the twentieth century, and it encapsulates the notion of the closing of one era and the onset of another.

As we shall see below, this has further implications when we consider this period as a response and reaction to the Romantic Period (and Romanticism itself) but seemingly, in Westernized cultures, this often meant a period of degeneracy and that by the actual turning point of the two centuries at 1900, much hope had disappeared, and in fact, emotions of ennui, cynicism and pessimism began to dominate; all issues which were perhaps then reinforced by the subsequent onset of the First World War. In this respect, the *Fin de Siècle* seemed to contain a notion that the development of so-called civilization led paradoxically to decadence.[93] This may seem somewhat dreary but at the same time, one can understand why certain writers and com-

---

91 For an overview, see Beckson 1981; Hext and Murray 2019; Rodensky 2006.
92 Robbins 1996; Jensen 994.
93 To an extent, the *Fin-de-Siècle* coincided with both the Celtic Twilight and Revival around Europe. See, for example, Ellis 1993, and Shaw 2019.

mentators felt this weariness. In some ways, it was entirely prophetic about what the twentieth century would bring.

Such an ideological belief has profound consequences in Symons' drama. We need to remember that the play (although written earlier) was not published until 1917 and thus the text physically emerged three years into the conflict of the Great War. The fictional war between Ireland and Cornwall appears to match the war between Germany and the Allies. As we shall see in this section, Symons was also a self-confessed champion of the Decadent Movement.[94] We see this aspects not only in the conflict between Ireland and Cornwall, but also in particular, in the Queen of Ireland's court where there is a pervasive sense of one "heroic" era collapsing around the characters after Tristan's killing of their warrior champion: the Morholt. Cynicism is found in the words of the Queen of Ireland who does not know what to do, and how to cope in this new era, whilst the pessimism is to be seen in the observations of Iseult of Ireland, who does not know what the future has in store for her. This is understandable since she is set to start her life in another country, in an arranged and political marriage to an older man.

The two characters who perhaps are better at embracing this new end of an era are Tristan himself, who is the force of decadent change in the text, alongside the observing Iseult of Brittany, who delights in the ennui offered by the collapse of Irish royalty. Clearly, in the long term, Symons shapes Iseult of Brittany as someone who hopes to benefit from the decadence now witnessed in the civilization around her: maybe therefore, it is her time, and later, she capitalizes upon this in her ensnaring of Tristan. The Decadent agenda would also appear to initially benefit Meriadoc, though he does capitulate to the old order at the end of Act One, in order to formulate his revenge. Eventually the reader learns that Meriadoc endures a moral breakdown leading to decadence manifested in violence. Thus the Decadent Movement enshrined in the text is revealed in such ways.

In general of course, Decadence of the kind to which Symons subscribed is perhaps seen as a movement following an aesthetic swing towards excess and artificiality. This all sounds very surface level and ungrounded, but in fact the movement (as Symons well knew) had

---

94 Boyiopoulos 2015; Bizzotto and Evangelista 2018.

broader aims and sympathies. It was characterized by valuing artifice over what was viewed as the Romanticism's naïve view of nature (itself a reaction to the Enlightenment).[95] Allied to this came self-disgust, an awareness of the sickness in the world, and a general scepticism over how society was progressing. The view was that Romanticism had not delivered. The bardic orders which were to follow in Wales (in 1861) and Cornwall (in 1928) were a case in point, both offering a somewhat flaccid reconstruction of an imagined heroic and ancient past.

One can see from this that such an agenda may have presented Symons with a problem in his imagining of Tristan and Iseult. In many ways, harking back to a Celtic romance was about a Romantic Period thing as one could do, and already the antiquarian agenda of Celtic Studies had aligned itself to Medievalism, heroism and chivalry;[96] all components which we might expect to see in a version of Tristan and Iseult, coupled, of course, with dramatic landscape, imaginings of childhood and an anti-industrial agenda. Celtic names (such as Meriadoc and Brangaene) as well as locations such as Tintagel and Brittany merely added to this). This gave Symons a difficulty since he needed to incorporate these Romantic Period aspects, but he wanted to also show the Decadence of such a world, reflecting the *Fin de Siècle* that he felt.

This paradox may actually be the reason why Symons' text is such a refreshing version of the story since the audience or reader can see these twin aspects competing for space in the play. Thus, in terms of the Decadent Movement Symons' *Tristan and Iseult* carries much delight in perversion (characters delighting in other characters suffering and feeling paralysis) and the employment of crude humour (though this can also be wildly symbolic). Crucial perhaps in the play is Symons' agenda that appears to have a belief in the superiority of human creativity over logic and the natural world (particularly seen in Tristan and Iseult's affair, and in Iseult of Brittany's machinations). Logic and the natural world would dictate therefore that Tristan and Iseult will not fall in love due to their social obligations, that, for example, Mark will kill, or harshly punish Tristan when he finds out about his affair with his wife, or even Iseult of Brittany's illogical

---

95 See Owens and Johnson 1998; Carruthers and Rawe 2003.
96 Williams 1971; Koch and Carey 1995.

and misguided understanding that she can make her "constructed" Tristan values her above and beyond his true love: Iseult of Ireland. We thus see in the play that art is totally opposed to nature in the sense of both biological nature and the standard norms of morality and sexual behaviour. Indeed, it may well have been Symons' overt agenda to push against the grain of the latter two issues and make audiences and readers realize the complex of morality and sexual behaviour in the new century. In point of fact, Symons may well have chosen Tristan and Iseult because its narrative offered exactly the right possibilities for confronting such issues.

At this point it may be worth discussing further how Decadence spread during this phase. Broadly, it first flourished in France (this would account for Symons' fascination with French writers such a Charles Baudelaire)[97] and then spread throughout continental Europe, and then to Great Britain and the United States of America. Such individuals even conceived of themselves as "Decadents" (with Symons almost imagining his Tristan as such an individual). This concept of decadence in fact is an earlier one, and dates from the eighteenth century, especially from Baron Montesquieu (Charles-Louis de Secondat) (1689–1755),[98] and was taken up by critics as a term of abuse after Désiré Nisard (1806–1888) used it against Victor Hugo and Romanticism in general.[99] A later generation of Romantics, such as Théophile Gautier (1811–1872),[100] and the aforementioned Baudelaire then took the word as a badge of pride, as a sign of their rejection of what they saw as banal progress. It is clear that Symons had empathy not only with the contemporary movement but that which also had been articulated earlier in the eighteenth century. His gaze (as can be seen in many of his critical writings) were to such writers. Certainly, in several sequences of Symons' play the influence of Baudelaire is pervasive at all times.

---

97 See Creasey 2014:165–9. See Clark 2004.

98 Baron Montesquieu (Charles-Louis de Secondat) was a French political philosopher. See Shackleton 1961.

99 Jean Marie Napoléon Désiré Nisard was a French author, literary critic and fierce opponent of Romanticism. See Chisholm 1911:709.

100 Gautier was a French poet, dramatist, novelist and literary critic. See Creasy 2014:156–61; Duncker and Constantine 2005 [1835].

Some further important strands may be alluded to here. In general, the Decadents were influenced by the tradition of the Gothic novel and as we shall next see, were usually associated alongside Symbolism and Aestheticism. These trends can usually be seen as fitting inside the wider genre of Decadent Movement, but at the same time they can exist independently from it. Symons triangulates the three in both his creative and critical output: a merging of trends deriving from his reading of earlier Decadent texts. Perhaps the first great Decadent work was Joris-Karl Huysman's novel *À rebours* [*Against Nature*] (1884) whose eccentric central character Jean des Esseintes retreats into a world of aestheticism and sensory experiences, contrary to the wishes of his family.[101] One can see the influence of such a work on Symons, in particular, in his own poetry but also the play under scrutiny here. For example, after her experience of dealing with the death of her uncle at the sword of Tristan in Act One, Iseult of Ireland seems to wish for the same kind of response, wanting to run from reality into aestheticism. Her view is only changed when she imbibes of the love potion, and ironically, it is then that she finds sensory experiences (both mental and physical) in her love for Tristan. Huysman's presence is felt in the play, and the influence of Baudelaire on Symons, and on the language of the play will be further considered below.

As the reader has probably realized by now, in Britain and Ireland, the leading figure associated with the Decadent Movement was Oscar Wilde (1854–1900).[102] Wilde, as Irish playwright, poet, novelist and essayist. Although few traces of Wilde's acerbic wit can be found in Symons' drama, he would have been aware of Wilde's decadent tendencies and how crucial these were in both encapsulating and confronting society at this time. It seems likely that Symons was sympathetic to Wilde's homosexuality (though perhaps had no interest in it), and there may in this be a nascent link between such cultural doubling, and that found of the twin Iseults and the relationship between Iseult of Ireland and Brangaene of Symons' play.[103]

---

101 McGuinness and Baldick 2003 [1884].

102 Cave 2000; Mighall 2003. For criticism, see Boyiopoulos, 2015. A fictional feel of the period is found in Ackroyd 1983. Oscar Wilde visited Cornwall on 5 November 1883. He spoke at Penzance Institute. See *Cornish Telegraph*. 8 November 1883:4 and 8.

103 For this LGBT strand, see March 1993, a novel which examines a Lesbian-themed

Certainly, Symons does push at the traditional boundaries of the way such heroic characters are presented.

Symons' dramaturgy will be explored later, but there is certainly a notion that he had a very focused interest in the design and feel of his play. Symons therefore seems aware of wider artistic and cultural movements in *Fin-de-Siècle* Europe. The artist and illustrator Audrey Beardsley (1872–1898) was another member of the Decadent Movement, who Symons was to write a study of.[104] Beardsley chose a style of illustration very influenced by Japanese art using black ink drawings and they were strongly erotic and sometimes grotesque. In the first phase of his career he designed illustrations for an edition of *Le Morte d'Arthur* by Thomas Malory, and it is not difficult to make a connection between what he was illustrating in the Arthurian world, and what Symons saw in the parallel universe of his Tristan and Iseult.[105] Beardsley was able to offer to Malory a certain decadence and mystical eroticism, which perhaps were also present in Symons' play. Visually therefore, there is perhaps much to be argued tor in terms of Symons wishing for an Beardsley-like imagining of his characters, stage design and set.

The other comparable figure in this group was Ernest Dowson (1867–1900).[106] Dowson was much admired by Symons, and was most successful as a poet and critic. He had less success as novelist (his two novels were co-written with Alan Moore), and he tried in his work to elucidate further the principles of the Decadent Movement. As a critic, Symons did much to promote and celebrate his work. Dawson was in the right position at the right time, though perhaps saw less contemporary success and fame than Wilde, and even

Tristan and Iseult narrative, with a female Tristan (Tristanne). Another interpretation is that the Lesbian issue is between Iseult and Brangain. See https://qlorgnette.wordpress .com/2020/04/25/invisible-lesbians-opera-edition accessed 2021-07-22. A Lesbian reading of traditional Tristan and Iseult narratives is possible, and also with Symons' 1917 play. In contemporary literary theory, this is often known as a form of dissident reading. For background, see Sinfield 1992.

104 Symons 1948 [1898].

105 For a detailed consideration of Beardsley's illustrations for *Le Morte d'Arthur* by Thomas Malory, see https://www.enchantedbooklet.com/le-morte-darthur accessed 2021-07-22. There are even some similarities in Beardsley's illustrations and those completed by Edmund Dulac for Yeats' play *At the Hawk's Well*. See Cave 1997:i; Dorn 1983.

106 See Ernest Dowson, *The Poems and Prose*, CreateSpace Independent Publishing Platform, 2017. See also Rodensky 2005, Boyiopoulos 2015.

Symons himself. Dowson remained more or less ignored for much of the twentieth century, but in recent years his work has also undergone something of a critical revival.[107] Dowson's and Symons' poetry have much in common and this is why he is given brief mention here.

From the dates of these other Decadents, it is easy to see that Symons was somewhat the last of their kind. This may account for much. It could be said that Symons represented the tail-end of the Decadent Movement and for that reason alone, this fact may have consigned him to relative obscurity. He was clearly operating at the other end of the cultural scale from other Celtic Revivalism in both Wales and Cornwall, and it may have been that the twain would never have met: a logical reason for why Cornish cultural activists of the twentieth appear to have lost sight of Symons' play. This was one reason for his cultural eclipse. The second arose from timing. Whilst Wilde, Beardsley and Dowson had been at the forefront of the movement's energy, Symons was somewhat late to the party. By the time he was active, literary tastes had changed and the energies of the Decadents had shifted into full-blown Modernism, embodied in the work of writers such as Knut Hamsun, Katherine Mansfield, James Joyce and Virginia Woolf. To this extent, this may offer us an insight into why Symons suffered such mental anguish and why works such as his decadent *Tristan and Iseult* play became lost. It is probable that if his *Tristan and Iseult* was published some twenty years earlier at the end of the nineteenth century, then it would have been a much more celebrated work both in English literary studies and those operating in Cornwall.

---

107 See, for example, Adams 2001; Jones 2019.

6

Symons' *Tristan and Iseult*: Continuity and Change

As we might expect, given Symons' influences and contemporaries (as discussed above), his dramatic version of *Tristan and Iseult* is loaded with heavy symbolism (Queen: "These wandering children of the harp, / Follow the crying people of the air"),[108] yet was intended to be performed with simple and intimate staging ("*the deck of* TRISTAN'*s ship, partly curtained off*").[109] However, this simplicity is counterpointed by the formality of both the poetic and ritualized speech and the intensity of the tragedy; with the work repudiating other early twentieth-century naturalism throughout. A summary of the plot is useful at this point, coupled with some observations on how Symons changed elements of the traditional narrative, which had evolved over several centuries of re-telling since the original Cornish version, as suggested by Jenner. The play is divided into four Acts: with Act I taking place in Ireland, Act II on the ship travelling from Ireland to Cornwall, Act III in Cornwall, and Act IV in Brittany.

Earlier Tristan narratives choose to start the telling of the story by having a conversation in Cornwall between King Mark and Tristan, explaining his mission to bring Iseult of Ireland to him to become his queen; and that in order to achieve this he may well have to defeat the Irish Champion Morholt, who has demanded tribute from Cornwall. In Symons' play, this part of the action is dispensed with and the audience enter the narrative in *media res*, where the Morholt has already been killed by Tristan. The Morholt is the Irish Queen's brother and we find her in discussion with her daughter Iseult and nephew Meriadoc over events (Meriadoc: "I speak another thing

---

108 I.2–3. References to lines in the play refer to Act and line number as given in the text beginning on p. 83.
109 II.1 s.d.

now. I desire / Vengeance for Morolt, blood for Morolt's blood").[110] Circumstances in Ireland have driven Iseult into madness, for she can barely conceive of what Tristan has done to her uncle, nor can she understand her fate in Cornwall. Her insecurities and fears are palpable and she is presented by Symons as being unsettled and almost mad ad psychotic (Iseult of Ireland: "What shall we do, mother? Oh, mother, tell me / Why could I not kill Tristan?").[111] The sequence concludes with dialogue (in imabic pentameter) between the King of Ireland, the Queen and Tristan:

QUEEN.
My lord, this grave and most unlooked-for thing,
Which sets my brother's slayer by my side,
Not at my feet, but honoured as a guest,
Brings not less strange a fellow with it. This,
Our enemy, comes from our enemy,   260
King Mark of Cornwall, he that harried us,
And now, being other minded, offers peace.

KING OF IRELAND.
I am well content to hold him for ally.

QUEEN.   More than ally.
He would become our kinsman, and desires   265
To bind us to his person, and has sent
His kinsman here to speak for him and ask
The hand of Iseult. Will you answer him?

KING OF IRELAND.
The hand of Iseult?

TRISTAN.   Even no less, my lord.
He is a king, but he is an old man,   270
And cannot go about the world and woo
A woman to his side.[112]

---

110 I.14–15. The usual spelling for the Morholt is with an h.
111 I.134–135.
112 I.256–272.

Two major changes are introduced here. Within the Irish court, the action is observed and commented on by Iseult of Brittany (generally known in the canon as "Iseult of the White Hands"). This structural placing of her here however, is a very astute move by Symons however, since it counters Iseult of the White Hands as a being a kind of odd coda figure as found in most established narratives. Thus the doppelgänger / double figure of Iseult of Brittany is witness to events in Ireland, and can observe how Iseult of Ireland first responds to Tristan. In this Act, Symons also introduces the newly-invented character of Meriadoc ("The splinter of the sword that killed my father. / Give it to me, and it shall draw the sword.").[113] As will be discussed below in more detail, this is a completely new character though whose name in reality has several legendary associations with Cornwall; this giving us our first understanding that either Symons knew the play of *Beunans Meriasek*, or was aware of the tradition in Camborne.

Surprisingly however, Symons then dismisses this Brythonic heritage and realigns the name and ethnicity of the character to Ireland. Meriadoc is therefore presented as a contender for marriage with Iseult of Ireland. He is the nephew of the Queen, and is therefore the Morholt's son. Throughout the Queen and Iseult's interrogation of Tristan, Meriadoc appears to be Iseult's protector, and when marriage is agreed with King Mark, only then does Meriadoc snidely appear to accept his position behind both the King and his nephew. Unbeknown to the audience however, he is plotting revenge on Tristan for both killing his father and for taking away the woman that he loves. The Meriadoc of Symons' play therefore is transitioned from being a Brythonic saint and confessor (initially Breton, then Cornish) into an Irish Machiavellian revenger ("the knife is ready for his throat.").[114]

Part of Symons' skills with Act One is the way he makes Iseult utterly dislike Tristan at this point. This hatred of him continues in Act Two as they set sail from Ireland to Cornwall. On board the ship Iseult is travelling with her confident and lady in waiting, Brangaene (usually Brangain). Brangaene is usually the figure who supplies the love potion to Tristan and Iseult to engender their affair.

113 I.44–45.
114 I.155.

Here, however, she has a more distant role, with Symons enhancing the innocence of Tristan and Iseult's love by having the cup of love potion provided to them by a naive Child (Iseult: "Where is the child / Who loves to wait upon me? Child! Bring me some wine, / A flagon, and a cup").[115] The effect of this is to decrease the emphasis on the manipulation of their affair and to suggest that their love is more natural. In this way, Symons also symbolically confronts any latent Christian additions to the narrative (the love potion is thought by many critics to have been added in order appease Christian readers over their affair). Thus, whilst at the start of the Act Tristan and Iseult dislike each other intently, by the end of it, they are planning to covertly meet each other in Tintagel. The drama makes overt their sexual decadence and willingness to subvert expectation. No more is heard of Iseult of Brittany at this point in the play.

In Act Three, we are introduced to King Mark himself who is accompanied by a character called Melot. Melot is Mark's fool at the court, but he is also his spy and henchman ("Because the moon called and the owlet called; / I looked out of my window... / I saw his footprints.").[116] Melot has spied Tristan meeting up with Iseult, but he has not actually seen them sleeping together. However, he infers as much to King Mark, who decides upon a course of action. Unknown to both Melot and Mark, their conversation is overheard by Tristan and Iseult who are hiding nearby and talk openly about their sexuality. Tintagel's isolation or "romance" seems to permit this. Therefore, they are prepared to be confronted by King Mark, with Iseult not fearing the repercussions of their affair, but with Tristan now more worried about his allegiance to his uncle and to Cornwall. When the confrontation comes, it is achieved in a very direct and logical way, with Iseult having to swear that she had not slept with Tristan, and Tristan being forced into exile overseas (Mark: "I banish you from Cornwall.").[117]

A jump in time and action is provided in Act Four. In this section we see Symons presenting an injured Tristan. At some point in the recent past he has been stabbed by Meriadoc with a poisoned-tipped dagger, and he is dying (Iseult of Brittany: "It was the poisoned knife

---

115 II.144–146.
116 III.16–17, 19.
117 III.317.

of Meriadoc.").[118] However, he is being cared for by Iseult of Brittany, who seemingly has taken pity on him, and loves him deeply despite him still longing for King Mark's wife. It seems this Iseult is prepared for this undercurrent of affection for the Iseult of Ireland as long as Tristan is in her life. This Act now puts her responses in Act One into perspective. As the Act proceeds however, the audience have to deal with the wrenching agony of Tristan calling out for Iseult of Ireland, while at times, Iseult of Brittany thinks he is calling for her. Tristan explains that if a ship arrives with a white sail, then it will carry his first love, Iseult of Ireland. There is a storm and the exterior tempest symbolically represents the relationship between Tristan and Iseult of Brittany.

Eventually, this jealousy affects Iseult of Brittany and she informs Tristan that a ship has arrived but that it has a black sail. The black sail symbolizes that Iseult of Ireland is not on board, and at this news, Tristan gives up the ghost and dies. Hating the fact that she has lied to him, Iseult of Brittany instantly corrects herself but it is now too late. She has already reflected on her actions:

He is all hers, but he is also mine.
Why should she come, being so rich to me   90
Who am so poor? Must beggars give back alms?
This man is mine, I hold him: better dead
And mine, than hers and living. What have I said?
It is this deadly woman whom I hate
That comes to bring him death...[119]

Iseult of Ireland then enters and she finds him dead ("He was the glory of the world; all the world's dust.").[120] She lies down with Tristan to comfort him and herself, and she then also dies. At the end of the Act, King Mark arrives to discover both of their bodies lying together but he realizes that he is too late, and following advice from Brangaene on their innocence, realizes that he is too late for

---

118 IV.28.
119 IV.89–95.
120 IV.315–316.

revenge. Like King Mark, Iseult of Brittany is destined to walk the earth alone ("Where shall I go? for I have killed my lord.").[121] The play ends with Mark calling for the bodies of Tristan and Iseult to be taken back to Tintagel.

---

121 IV.313.

7

The Transformation of Meriadoc: From Saint to Sinner

In Symons' creation of his version of *Tristan and Iseult*, a core puzzle remains as to why he selected Meriadoc as the name for his Irish revenger. On the face of it, the name Meriadoc was once virtually unknown outside of Cornwall, but illumination from elsewhere may go at least some way to explain why Symons selected it. That illumination is found in the work of Carl Phelpstead in his 2011 study *Tolkien and Wales: Language, Literature and Identity*.[122] Phelpstead's study counters much traditional Tolkien criticism which suggests that J. R. R. Tolkien (1892–1973) was inspired to write his texts *The Hobbit* (1937) and *Lord of the Rings* (1954–1955) by using mainly Anglo-Saxon and Scandinavian sources to inspire his shaping of Middle Earth.[123] In fact, Tolkien additionally integrated many Celtic sources into the world he created, and it is this aspect that Phelpstead explores in his argument, not only examining purely Welsh sources, but also those from Brittany and Cornwall. His volume is not solely about Wales but actually about Brythonic Celtic culture.

Two core aspects emerge from this. According to Phelpstead it appears that Tolkien once owned what is described as an "uncut" edition of Whitley Stoke's 1872 translation of *Beunans Meriasek [The life of Meriadoc]*, so he was at least somewhat aware of the name.[124] It is thus suggested that he used the name to inspire one of the hobbits created as part of the Fellowship of the Ring: that of Merry Brandybuck. Merry Brandybuck's full name is Meriadoc Brandybuck. Thus clearly, Tolkien was just as interested in the name as Symons was.

---

122 Phelpstead 2011.
123 Burns, 2005. Despite this volume's title the pre-eminent focus in this volume is on Norse heritage.
124 Phelpstead 2011:130.

Perhaps not coincidentally, the name Rohan is also found in the Cornish-language miracle play,[125] and it is argued that this too, formed the inspiration for Tolkien's kingdom of horsemen.

What are we to make of this? On one level it might suggest that Stokes' edition of *Beunans Meriasek* travelled further into English and non-Celtic culture than we first might believe. Stokes' text however, had come out almost forty years before Tolkien and Symons were writing. It is, of course, more conceivable that Tolkien might encounter a copy in his capacity as an academic, though when Symons was publishing his play Tolkien was still serving as a fusilier in World War One. Tolkien therefore, had to encounter it much later. Symons, on the other hand, was clearly either aware of the text and the name much earlier on. Could it have been that his parents purchased a copy of Stokes' edition closer to its publication, and then this found its way into Symons' hands? This seems unlikely as the text was obscure with limited print run.

There may well have been some other methods of transition however. Symons may well have been aware of the volume through his work as a critic. His association with Yeats may have brought Stokes (as a scholar of Celtic literature) to his attention, with an off-hand observation that there existed a Cornish-language text. Alternatively, lots of texts would have been passed his way, and presumably he kept an eye out for Cornish and Welsh-related material considering his personal heritage. Stokes' volume may well have come across his desk in some capacity and when thinking through the revenger character in his proposed play, he deemed the name interesting and appropriate (in exactly the same way that Tolkien was to do). Maybe in the names Morholt and Meriadoc he saw a semi-alliterative connection. Needless to say, unlike Tolkien, Symons had no understanding of Brythonic linguistics and did not think through this, when it came to naming an Irish character with a Cornish/Breton name.

Other possibilities exist however. It might have been that Symons' parents had some distant connection with Camborne and one of its patron saints and that he would have grown up being aware of the

---

125 Stokes 1872:124–5. New and revised translations of the text are offered by Combellack 1988; Chubb 2018. Chubb's translation makes considerable revision to that originally offered by Stokes.

name because it was part of his family's culture.[126] This seems distinctly unlikely though given that the two sides of the family were from mid and North Cornwall. It might also have been prompted by a prior holiday or journey back to Cornwall, though this excursion or connection to Camborne is not mentioned by Symons' biographers or in his correspondence. Indeed, in a volume that sought to re-assert Celtic naming culture in Cornwall, a book published in 1984 argues that Meriadoc and Meriasek are traditional names for the Cornish,[127] though this is perhaps wishful thinking, since it seems highly unlikely that anyone at the turn of the twentieth century would be named in such a manner and that the volume was published only to address the needs of revivalist and nationalistic parents in Cornwall who sought to re-engage with Celtic heritage.

In looking for possibilities, there are also a series of 48 booklets published by Gilbert H. Doble (1880–1945) who documented the lives of well-known saints in Cornwall. These were later assembled into complete volumes. In one volume Doble considers in detail the *vitae* and associations of Meriadoc.[128] Such a volume might also seems to be a likely place where Symons might have drawn the name, but unfortunately this also yields us a dead end, since Doble only published his volumes from 1923 onwards, some six years after the emergence of Symons' play and a long time after his drafting of it. Unless Doble (who would have been aged just 27) and Symons were in correspondence, then once more this seems an unlikely route for the name's derivation and its eventual integration.

There is perhaps one more avenue we may consider. It is specifically related to the period in which Symons was drafting *Tristan and Iseult*. We have already considered the possibility of him encountering Stoke's translation of the play, but in 1904 Henry Jenner finally published his groundbreaking *Handbook of the Cornish Language*, which was not only the first modern textbook on how to learn the language but also gave an account of the historical literature in Cornish. In the section of the book titled "The Literature and Other Remains of Cornish" Jenner gives an account of *Beunans Meriasek*, noting that

126 For background, see Thomas1967.
127 Anonymous 1984:30.
128 Doble 1997:111–45.

the name in Breton would be Meriadoc.[129] There is strong possibility that Symons would have noted Jenner's volume and purchased a copy, but in his correspondence there is no mention of it. However, given the date, it completely fits Symons' development of the text.

It could be however, that a combination of many of these possible sources worked on Symons' imagination, and that somehow the half-remembered name was considered suitable for his purpose. Williams has recently argued for the transformative nature of Irish gods, pagan deities and saints, and recognizes that each new generation reinterprets particular names and figures for their own cultural purpose, despite sometimes going against the overwhelming textual and historical evidence.[130] In microcosm, the very same thing may well be happening here and it has to be said that in the wider scheme of things there is no reason why Symons might select a past name to be reprocessed and reconfigured, and to transform a Celtic saint into a weaponized and revenging sinner.

With our Celtic Studies eye we may now find the application of a Brythonic name onto a broadly Gaelic culture to be inexplicable but it is perhaps no more inexplicable than conveniently having a Breton woman (Iseult of the White Hands) at the Queen of Ireland's court. In the wider scheme of things it would perhaps be unlikely that readers or audiences of Symons' play would have even noticed such cultural and linguistic problems. For them, it is likely the name would have somehow sounded weird and ancient, and therefore conveniently "Celtic". Maybe too, this was all that Symons wanted to achieve and that his more urgent need was put into his depiction of decadence and madness within the play.

---

129 Everson 2010:28. Symons would surely have known of the work of Whitley Stokes and perhaps some of the other figures in the Celtic Revival in Cornwall, including Henry Jenner. There is a vast quantity of Henry Jenner letters held at the British Library which need to be scrutinised further to determine any correspondence between them. Symons was aware of the importance of minority languages and literatures however. For example, an acquaintance was the Provençal poet and playwright Joseph Roumanille (1829–1940). He and others were interested in restoring Provençal as a literary language. Symons notes this in a letter to Katherine Willard, 20 May 1981, MS Baldwin. See Beckson and Monro, 2015:79–80.

130 Williams 2016:434–88. Williams also argues for Tolkien's integration of Gaelic culture into his legendarium. See pp. 475–6.

8

A Vision of Decadence: Symons' Suggestive Tintagel

Frustrating as it is, we shall probably never fully know why Symons integrated the name Meriadoc into his drama, and it remains a tantalizing curiosity. As indicated above, there are many moments in Symons' text, where on both a macro and micro level Symons incorporates symbolism. Some contemporary readers might view these as sometimes clumsy but in his wider work, Symons was trying to push the capabilities of literature and progress to a new way of writing and reading that was less linked to literary "social" realism. Compared to many of the established versions of the narrative, Symons' version is much more erotic and decadent; and at the same time, sexually nuanced as the love of Tristan and Iseult is "watched" by Mark and his fool Melot. In effect, Symons's suggestively positions them as voyeurs in the environment of the castle at Tintagel.

Melot in particular, notices every gesture the lovers make and gives it sexual credence. When he describes Tristan "entreating something" Mark sees this as a "wild jest" questioning if she was "flushed" (an indication of sexualized excitement). Melot's response is that in fact they were "paler, and both as if some hunger / Starved both their faces thin"[131] which also lends itself to be symbolically interpreted as sexual frustration. There is also much symbolic discussion of "flame on flame"—suggestive of copulation and the sexual act itself, with Melot working on Mark much in the same way as Iago does on Othello in Shakespeare's drama. One term used is the word "thrust" which again gives an audience the impression of frenzied sexual activity.[132] Unlike Tristan, Mark and Merlot are cynical about the ways and wiles of women, a conversation that conclude with

---

131 III.36–37.
132 III.71, 73.

Symons' Mark saying, "Death is a woman and plays / A secret game with us".[133] The wider tone is that Iseult is behaving like a whore (very much like Desdemona in *Othello*), even though Mark wants to believe that this would be "unthinkable".[134] The audience however, already knows that it is not.

When the action turns to Tristan and Iseult themselves, their conversation is again sexualized. Tristan says, "Have I not held your body with my hands? / Have I not drunk your soul up with my lips?"[135] When the rosebush is discussed (an established icon in the corpus), it is metaphorically transitioned into something symbolic of sexual orgasm and that this is best seized upon in the here and now, for neither of the lovers know their fate: "These roses are the prodigals of June, / They burn, they waste to ashes, they are a fire".[136] This culminates in the animalistic desire of Iseult who says, "O I would be a beast and eat your lips".[137] It is perhaps no wonder with a text such as this that Symons was aware of issue of censorship upon the stage, and for truth and consistency often sought to mount his drama outside of Britain so as not to see his work bowdlerized or altered. When one considers this sexualized Tintagel, we need to bear in mind that elsewhere in Britain in general audiences were still lapping up the sentimental and inoffensive comedies of conservative writers such as Arthur Wing Pinero (1855–1934).[138]

Symons is doing something much more ambitious here, and as can be seen from above, his cues were not contemporary writers like Pinero; rathermore, it was coming from Shakespeare himself, who Symons seems to regard as a master of symbolism. Sexual "honour", for example is shockingly described by Iseult of Ireland as "that barren bastard word / Honour".[139] Similarly the adultery is confronted head on, with Iseult's frustration at their parting coupled with the line "Tristan, this is my body and my blood, / And they are yours".[140] Iseult speaks her lines in an almost ritualistic manner,

---

133 III.85–86.
134 III.88.
135 III.93–94.
136 III.105–106.
137 III.135.
138 Wyatt 1985.
139 III.175–176.
140 III.189–190.

pleading for sexual contact between them. In such lines we see that Symons was consciously trying to depict women in a more realistic way (his contact with Havelock Ellis made him progressively understand women's sexuality). Still however, such matters were not to be discussed on stage, a view reflected in the admonitions made by Iseult's lady-in-waiting Brangaene, who at her lady's shocking sexual openness chides her with "Mistress!"[141] Maybe observers and producers of the work felt this was too sexually radical and is the reason why the work was not produced in Rome or elsewhere.

In comparison to the earlier depiction of Ireland, and the future representation of Brittany, Tintagel is therefore presented as more sexually decadent and in a way, freer and more open. Perhaps Symons was aware of the other sexual deviancy of the Arthurian corpus in Cornwall in the form of Uther Pendragon disguising himself as Gorlois, the Duke of Cornwall (at Tintagel) in order to make love with Igraine, culminating in the birth of Arthur, as well as the later affair of Mordred and Guinevere, both going against Arthur (not usually at Tintagel but often set in a Cornu-Celtic landscape).[142] Undoubtedly, a comparison of symbolism used by Thomas Hardy and Arthur Symons in their respective imaginings of Tristan, Iseult and Tintagel should be completed, but it is one that will have to wait for another time. Suffice to say, that both writers embed their tellings with symbol and allegory. With the former, some observers have gone so far to suggest that the Iseult of Ireland and the Iseult of Brittany represent Hardy's two wives, Emma Gifford and Florence Dugdale.[143] Further scrutiny of Symons' own relationships might result in just such a reading of his version.[144]

A reading of Yeats' plays in Cave's collection demonstrates to us that Symons' drama has very similar characteristics, particularly in terms of the openness and frankness in which women's sexuality and affairs are presented. Yeats drew on mythological sources for much

---

141 II.114.

142 Bodmin Moor is often positioned, and in some accounts Goss Moor. With the latter, the final battle is often constructed as being fought between Castle-an-Dinas and St Dinas (another hill-fort).

143 See Phelps 1975.

144 I say this with extreme caution. See my earlier observations about such biographical criticism.

of his work, but the same issues face his characters—where he wants to challenge convention and articulate a symbolic "Celtic" world. Thus in plays such as *Cathleen ni Houlihan, On Baile's Strand, At the Hawk's Well,* and *The Death of Cuchulain* we see a comparable energy to that found in this single work by Symons.[145] Indeed, it would not be difficult to easily see *Tristan and Iseult* being one of Yeats' own dramas from this period.

---

145 See Cave 1997:19–29, 49–73, 113–24 and 263–72.

9

All Salt and Honey: Symons' Anglo-Cornish Poetry

This volume has shown throughout that Symons used his identity and time spent in Cornwall to develop Anglo-Cornish verse. This verse will now be given more detailed consideration. It is clear that by 1904 (four years before his mental breakdown) Symons was aware of the power of Cornwall on helping him to construct his poetry. Importantly, he shares this experience with—of all people—Thomas Hardy on 4 September, that year. We learn that Symons is at Poltescoe near Ruan Minor on the tip of the Lizard Peninsula.[146] Symons has been reading Hardy's novel *Jude the Obscure* which he describes as a "great book... so fine, so solid, so complete"[147] but also informs him of how inspirational the landscape and culture has been to him. Thus Symons writes:

> We have been here since the middle of July and are staying for nearly another month, in a thatched cottage at the very end of Cornwall, not far from the Lizard, ten miles form the railway, in a luxuriant valley close to the sea. The air is all salt and honey. I find myself writing more verse than I have written all the time I was abroad.[148]

Here he seems to want Hardy to understand how the isolation of the peninsula is inspiring new work, though perhaps of all people, he had no need to tell Hardy this. Hardy himself was about to have his own final reconnection with Cornwall, not least in the form of

---

146 Poltescoe was one of the centres for the serpentine industry. See Kent 2019.
147 Letter to Thomas Hardy, 1 September 1904, MS., Dorset. Cited in Beckson and Monro 2015:172–3.
148 Letter to Thomas Hardy, 1 September 1904, MS., Dorset. Cited in Beckson and Monro 2015:172–3.

his own late Emma Gifford poems (most set in the landscape around Boscastle) and his version of the story of *Tristan and Iseult*. However, his correspondence with Symons does make us wonder whether Hardy himself became influenced by Symons' own earlier interest in the Tristan corpus, before his own take on the story began to emerge. Likewise, Symons' reconnection with Cornwall during this phase might even have stimulated Hardy's own reflection on his earlier relationship with Emma. Whatever we may think, there is a tantalizing link between the two poets operating at the same time, and using very similar base material for their work.

Most of Symons' poetry intersects with Symbolist reflections on morality, love and death. In assessing it we see that there are the occasional longer deviations into Classical legend or Biblical narrative where he believes learning and "interpretation" can be derived from such stories. The Modernism in Symons' verse is derived from its sparse nature and its usual refusal either to conform to the conventions of rhyme or to subvert them. There is an emphasis on the senses though these are usually overhauled and presented in unconventional ways. The poems are often short and disavow traditional forms. There is a noticeable absence of a clear location because Symons' was mainly to focus on intuition and emotion. Very often, his poems reflect fully the notion of the tormented soul coming to terms with modernity and change, and often the poems consider the darker side of nature. The apparent absence of place may well be a problem for us in terms of relating his work to Cornwall, though thankfully despite this minimalism there is still enough work to show his connection and understanding. Continental European destinations, as we might expect, are marked more overtly, and there is also overt recognition of Irish place-names.[149]

The pervasive critical view of Symons was that he was at his most interesting in the volume *London Nights* (1895), where he was depicting the fairyland and light fantastic world of theatre and musical hall,

---

149 See Symons 1902, Vol 2., pp. 164–5. The sequence here is titled 'By Lough-na-Gar'. Despite extensive research however, I was unable to pin down this precise location. Nicholas Williams agrees with me that Symons probably took the name from the famous Irish folk song. There is, however, a place called *Loch na gCaor* which translates to 'the lake of the berries' in West Galway and Symons may well have used an anglicized spelling.

coupled perhaps with the city's seedier side. It is a theme which connects with the view that Symons' madness was a direct result of him hing syphilis, for it was a world which he partook of fully. Holdsworth rightly argues that Symons was the first poet to bring realistic pictures of relations with prostitutes into poetry and "so too, the imagery which accompanies this theme: cigarettes, macquillage [cosmetics], tumbled beds and scented boudoirs, none had appeared in English poetry before".[150] However this was not the full extent of Symons' work. In Volume One of his *Poems*, we do see some Cornish-themed poems, and in general these do seem to reflect moments in Symons' life. The whole of St Ives Bay is very memorable to him because of his early experiences there, and the time spent in Cornwall with Havelock Ellis. Therefore, we might expect a poem to document this experience, and "Carbis Bay" is that poem, with content here reinforced by the unusual rhyme scheme. Perhaps the most evocative line here is the way in which he describes Cornwall as being "the menace of the land", shifting the emphasis away from the potential danger of the sea to the threat of the landscape (something which the Anglo-Cornish literary scholar John Hurst recognized as being typically Cornish):[151]

> Out of the night of the sea,
> Out of the turbulent night,
> A sharp and hurrying wind
> Scourges the waters white:
> The terror by night.
>
> Out of the doubtful dark,
> Out of the night of the land,
> What is it breathes and broods,
> Hoveringly at hand?
> The menace of land.
>
> Out of the night of heaven,
> Out of the delicate sky,
> Pale and serene the stars

---

150 Holdsworth 2003:13.
151 Hurst 1993:291–308.

In their silence reply:
The peace of the sky.[152]

In another poem, "By Loe Pool" (1906), Symons moves to the southern coast of Cornwall to examine the lake at Loe Pool, near Porthleven, which was created by the tidal shifts of sands. There is an interesting line here ("And the cows coming down to the water one by one") which is an earlier recognitions of a point later again made by the Hurst, about the work of John Betjeman (1906–1984) in expressing that only in Cornwall would you find such an image. It seems to have had as much effect here on Symons as it later did on Betjeman.[153] The final line here is typical Symons, reiterating an earlier image, but leaving an unsettling feeling and almost a claustrophobic sensation with the freedom of the sea at Loe Pool being so close and yet so distant because of the sand bar:

> The pool glitters, the fishes leap in the sun
> With joyous fins, and dive in the pool again;
> I see the corn in sheaves, and the harvestmen,
> And the cows coming down to the water one by one.
> Dragon-flies mailed in lapis and malachite
> Flash through the bending reeds and blaze on the pool;
> Sea-ward, where trees cluster, the shadow is cool;
> I hear a sighing, where the sea is, out of sight;
> It is noontide, and the fishes leap in the pool.[154]

By now we recognize some of the pattern of the work and the way in which Symons constructs Cornwall. In many respects "Before The Squall" is a typical poem of this era about Cornwall, noting the growing atmospheric tension as a storm grows our at sea. However, the second verse adds a new dimension to such work, with Symons almost offering an image of a blacksmith as work, bending and shaping the landscape. The penultimate line which speaks of "Grey in

---

152 Symons 1902, Vol 1, p. 103.

153 Hurst 1993. Hurst recounts Betjeman's lines "hilltops upon whose clinging sides the farms / Hold Bible Christians". See Betjeman 1960:53.

154 Symons 1906:37. This volume also includes the Cornish-themed poems "Songs of Poltescoe Valley", "To a Sea-Gull", and "Cornish Wind". See pp. 27–36.

the offing" is surely a weather condition that anyone who has spent time in Cornwall will know intimately: Yet the sails "that fly" seem to offer "honey" over and above the "salt" of the squall:

> The wind is rising on the sea,
> The windy white foam-dancers leap;
> And the sea moans uneasily,
> And turns to sleep, and cannot sleep.
>
> Ridge after rocky ridge uplifts,
> Wild hands, and hammers at the land,
> Scatters in liquid dust, and drifts
> To death among the dusty sand.
>
> On the horizon's nearing line,
> Where the sky rests, a visible wall,
> Grey in the offing, I divine,
> The sails that fly before the squall.[155]

Another early poem, "The Fisher's Widow" is a somewhat surprising work in Symons' canon of writing about Cornwall. It is more socially realist, conveying the heartache brought about by the danger of the fishing profession, and in a way, seems to be from an earlier phase of Anglo-Cornish poetry, and is not in alignment with Symons' usual concerns. Indeed, this fits because the poem was from Symons' Browingnesque phase originally in the volume *Days and Nights* (1889). There seems even a dose of sentimentality with him realizing that not all vessels safely return to harbour:

> She sees the torn sails fly in the foam,
> Broad on the sky-line gray;
> And the boats go out and the boats come in,
> But there's one away.[156]

---

155 Symons 1902, Vol. 1, p. 18.
156 Symons 1902, Vol. 1, p. 11. Browning was an important early influence on Symons. See Beckson and Munro 1970:687–699. *Cf.* the Browning influence on Jack Clemo. Yeats was also aware of the Browning influence but more sceptical about Symons being part of the Decadent Movement. He says that "what the public calls and condemns as

The second volume of *Poems* perhaps offers us sparser offerings than in the first. However pieces such as "In the Bay" are again surely depictions of Symons' experiences at St Ives or Carbis Bay: a combination of childhood memory and visitation as an adult:

> The sea-gulls whiten and dip,
> Crying their lonely cry,
> At noon in the blue of the bay;
> And I hear the slow oars drip,
> As the fisherman's boat drifts by,
> And the cuckoo calls from the hillside far away.[157]

Line six here is of note for the cuckoo is an unusual incorporation and it seems to suggest Symons' familiarity with the legend of the "The Cuckoo Feast" in the parish of Towednack in the hills above St Ives.[158] The poem continues along these lines, but at the end, Symons seems to wish for familiarity, and it is maybe Cornwall that offers it when he writes of death which is a journey, "To a shore far over the sea, / And I would that m ship went down within sight of the shore!"[159] This is powerful ending, and elsewhere he maintains Irish / Cornish interest in the poem "Modern Beauty" by referring once more to a familiar legendary figure:

> I am Yseult and Helen, I have seen
> Troy burn, and the most loving knight lie dead.

'decadence' is a rejection of the great impersonal themes of Tennyson and Browning" and "a calling of what is personal and solitary to the seat of song... One may say of Mr Symons that he is in no sense of the word a 'decadent', but a writer who has carried further than most of his contemporaries that revolt against the manifold, the impersonal, the luxuriant, and the external, which is perhaps the great movement of our time, and of more even than literary importance". See W. B. Yeats, "Mr Arthur Symons' new book [Review of *Amoris Victima*]" in *The Bookman*, April 1897. Cited in Frayne and Johnson 1975:38–42.

157 Symons 1902, Vol 2., p. 19.

158 It is probable that Symons heard of the legend of "The Cuckoo Feast". It is said that one cold April day a local farmer placed a large log on his hearth to warm himself when a cuckoo flew out from the inside the log, loudly calling "cuckoo". The farmer caught the bird and placed it in a cage, gathering his friends and a number of musicians to join him in parading the bird around the village in celebration. For an account, see Hunt *(Second Series)* 1865:404.

159 Symons 1902, Vol 2.

> The world has been my mirror, time has been
> My breath upon the grass; and men have said,
> Age after age, in rapture and despair,
> Love's poor few words, before my image there.[160]

Here Iseult is given the same status as Helen of Troy, which is praise indeed, and is obviously how Symons imagined his version of her. The main symbolism of the work contains the idea that such beauty all too often revolves like moths around a flame. In the end, Symons concludes "Still am I the torch, but where's the moth that still dares die?"[161] The suggestion is that death has not yet been completed because figures such as Iseult and Helen of Tory live on in legend. Despite the pull of the flame, Symons appears to suggest, they cannot die.

Another later poem titled "Wind on the Sea" makes a symbolic connection between the loneliness of life and the weather system around the observer. This is a very Baudelaire-type reflection on experience, which perhaps gives an impression of some of Symons' doubts and fears. It is harder of course, to say there is a direct link to Cornish experience, but by now we can note a pattern in his writing that when the sea is used symbolically it usually relates to experiences in the territory:

> The loneliness of my heart is in the sea,
> And my mind is not more lonely than the grey wind.
> Who shall stay at the feet of the sea, or bind
> The wings of the wind? Only the feet of mankind
> Grow old in the place of their sorrow, and bitter is the heart
> That may not wander as the wind or return as the sea.[162]

To this reader, such lines very much recall the verse of Katherine Lee Jenner,[163] who shows a similar symbolic fascination with the sea

---

160 Symons 1902, Vol 2, p. 150. There are numerous legendary associations attached to the connection between the founding of Cornwall and Trojan War refugees. It is curious why Symons selected to spell Iseult differently here than in his play.

161 Symons 1902, Vol 2.

162 Symons 1902, Vol 2, p. 183.

163 For poetry see Kent 2000:162–6. For criticism, see Kent in Williams 2004:119–57.

but who was not writing in the same tradition as Symons. It may be, of course, that the sea would always be an appropriate image for writers like Symons and Jenner who were essentially part of the Celtic *Fin de Siècle*. The line "Grow old in the place of their sorrow" is particularly effective though, and seems to resonate with Cornish experience over time, though of course, this may well not have been Symons' specific intention. Certainly this metaphor pattern much of the feeling during the Celtic Twilight or *Fin de Siècle* and that lamentation for what had been lost was the only way for poets to proceed.

10

Yeats and Symons: Who made who?

When considering Yeats' poetry and that by Symons side-by-side there is an interesting debate as to who influenced who. In most criticism (and because of the perceived greatness of Yeats' work, not to mention the dominance of Irish literary strudies)[164] in general, it is often Years who is positioned as influencing Symons. Certainly by the time Yeats was a successful and prolific Anglo-Irish poet, he had left Symons way behind. However, there is a good argument that, in fact, during Yeats' development phase, Symons' poetry and his criticism had a good deal of effect on Yeats.[165] There is not the space here to go into a full comparison of their early work but certainly one can see many symbolic comparisons between them, and early on, Yeats was certainly writing in the slip-stream of Symons. This changed later on however, with Yeats taking the lead in how he was dramatically presenting Ireland, and Symons saw much potential in

---

164 See Jefferies 1990. For a range of criticism, see Howes 2006. In his letters Symons makes notes of Iseult Gonne (1894–1953) who was the illegitimate daughter of Maud Gonne (1866–1953), whom Yeats loved and made the subject of many of his poems. See Letter to John Quinn, 7 September 1921, MS. Quinn, cited in Beckson and Munro 2015:248–9.

165 See, for example, an early review of Yeats by Symons. Anonymous [Arthur Symons]. 1903 in the *Athenaeum*, 27 June 1903. A more detailed comparison of the two is needed. One might consider the example of the identification of dancer and dance in Symons' "Nora" however, and how this becomes the "How can we tell the dancer from the dance" of Yeats' "Among School Children". This is perhaps proof of Symons' lasting influence. There is also a similarity between the opening lines of Symons' "La Mélinite": "Oliver Metra's Waltz of Roses / Sheds in a rhythmic shower / The very petals of the flower" and Yeats' "When Loie Fuller's Chinese dancers enwound": "It seemed that a dragon of air / Had fallen among dancers, had whirled them round / Or hurried them off on its on furious path." I am much indebted to Peter Brooke for pointing out these comparisons to me.

this. It is certainly the reason why Symons' *Tristan and Iseult* almost feels like reading an undiscovered Yeats' play.

Image: Arthur Symons, St. John's Wood, 22 September 1906.
Aged 41. Photographer: Alvin Langdon Coburn.

11
Symons and the Internet: A New On-line Spirituality

It appears that his twenty years of isolation offered Symons a chance to review and reflect on the Decadent Movement he was once such a central part of. Although apparently unnoticed as we shall see below in the observations of John Betjeman, Symons' wife Rhoda recognized that he had changed, and that by 1933 she was dealing with a very different individual. Maybe his literary disappointments or his madness had prompted a shift. Certainly he was more conscious of his sinfulness and his own imperfections, though in a letter to him Rhoda upbraided him for his feelings of moral and spiritual inadequacy (issues perhaps which in essence had beleaguered him throughout his life. She pertinently observes the following:

> If you realise *acutely* that you are an *eternal, perfect* expression
> of God—that realisation—if it is complete enough—is
> bound to cure you—keep consciously in your consciousness
> that you are now—always were—and always will be a son
> of God, therefore—*necessarily* perfect. That's what the Greeks
> meant when they wrote 'Know thyself'. The constant reali-
> sation that *Now* are we the Sons of God brings healing.
> Where the Spirit of the Lord is there is liberty' – (Liberty
> from disease and happiness).[166]

Despite the Christian overlay here, the sentiment is actually rather "New Age" in feel and although Rhoda could not have possibly predicted this, a simple search of the internet with show that in spite of

---

166 This is found in an MS., *c.*1933 from Columbia. The words that are in italics are underlined twice by Rhoda Symons. The quotation in brackets is from 2 Corinthians 3:17. Cited in Beckson and Monro 1989:203.

his Decadent Movement credentials that there are many memes and images quoting Symons' poetry and criticism to be found on the world-wide web, demonstrating that Symons' poetry is not now neglected and that its symbolic energy has been reprocessed for the "Self-Help" on on-line community.[167] Examples would be too numerous to quote here, and would not display the range of Symons' work that is used. However, any Image search on a regular Search Engine will provided the reader with a wide range of Symons' wisdoms and insights, and he speaks to us from cyberspace with a kind of Celtic-tinged wisdom, which he could never have imagined. Whilst Symons' poetry has rather been brushed aside by previous generations, it was finding a new place on the Internet.

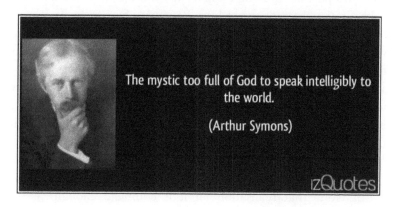

The mystic too full of God to speak intelligibly to the world.

(Arthur Symons)

izQuotes

---

167 See for example, https://izquotes.com/quotes-pictures/quote-the-mystic-too-full-of-god-to-speak-intelligibly-to-the-world-arthur-symons-270922.jpg shown above. Accessed 2021-07-22. It is entirely possible that some observers were making the connection between Yeats and Symons, as Yeats' poetry is often used in a similar way.

12

Cornwall Connected:
Betjeman on Symons

Symons' life and work may be summarized by a reaction to the non-conformist (and here, Wesleyan) upbringing he endured under his father, Mark Symons. This places Symons in a curious comparable position with many other significant Anglo-Cornish writers, including Jack Clemo, K. C. Phillips, D. M. Thomas and myself.[168] Although clearly Symons clashed with his father in the early part of his adult life, and hence his desire to escape austere Methodism and embrace decadent London and cosmopolitan continental Europe, towards the middle of his life, there was obviously some reconciliation as his father bequeathed his will to his son.[169] Although nonconformity carried its own set of symbols, it may well have seemed curiously out of step with the kind of Modernist symbolism that Symons wished to pursue in his poetry and drama, and is embodied in the poems discussed here, as well as his dramatization of *Tristan and Iseult*.

As this article has shown, although many observers and websites comment on Symons' identity as being Welsh,[170] he saw it as some-what different, and reiterated his Cornish identity throughout his life. It was pervasive during his discussions with Yeats over Celtic identity, and was still present in his conceptualization of the Tristan narrative. It was also present in many of the poems that he wrote, though perhaps unfortunately these were not the ones that were most noticed by the English literary establishment. Curiously too, Cornwall itself has seemingly been reluctant to claim Symons as its

---

168 Clemo 1975 [1949]; Phillips 1993; Thomas 1983; Kent 2010.
169 See in Beckson and Monro 1989:145. In a letter to Rhoda Bowser dated 4 March 1900, Symons explains that his father left him half of the money he had saved. Presumably the other half went to his sister, who is not much mentioned by Symons. It seems they fell out early on.
170 Most on-line entries about him describe Symons as being Welsh.

own.[171] This marks a problem with literary history in Cornwall, and with its obsessions and icons which are very often exaggerated out of all proportion compared to certain writers actual achievements.[172] Cornwall seems sometimes incapable of reassessing its own cultural and literary history, too often following well-worn paths of both text and authors: a legacy all too often embodied in the various literary festivals and promotional materials found around the territory.

One writer however, who is rightly positioned within the Anglo-Cornish canon of writing is John Betjeman. Cornwall was to remain a crucial influence in his work throughout his career, and in particular, he drew on the landscape and culture of North Cornwall, and his historic hagiographic heritage to assemble a depiction of a modern Cornwall enduring great change and transition, broadly under the shackles of tourism and development.[173] Payton, in his 2010 study of Betjeman, reasserts the poet's Cornish credentials, arguing with new evidence and insight that, in fact, Betjeman was definitively a "Cornish Nationalist".[174] In particular, it is through the lens of saints such as St Enodoc, St Cadoc and St Minver that Betjeman uses to construct his poet imagining of Cornwall, and so too, it is with Symons in his forthright re-imagining of St Meriadoc.

This was not the only collision between Betjeman and Symons. In *c.*1935, as Betjeman was writing poems that would eventually form his 1940 collection, *Old Lights for New Chancels*, he wrote a poem titled "On Seeing an Old Poet in the Café Royal":

> I saw him in the Café Royal
> Very old and very grand.
> Modernistic shone the lamplight
> There in London's fairyland.
> "Devilled chicken. Devilled whitebait.
> Devil if I understand.[175]

---

171 I have found no single source of literary criticism concerning Cornwall which mentions Symons.

172 Most popular studies exaggerate the significance of writers such as Daphne du Maurier, Winston Graham and Patrick Gale. Unlike Ireland, contemporary writers and ethnically Cornish writers are given little attention. As an example, see Kittow, 2015.

173 For an assessment, see Kent 2000:219–21.

174 Payton 2010.

175 Betjeman 1990:48. The Café Royal was one of Symons' favourites haunts. Down on his

The poet who Betjeman was observing was Arthur Symons, who by now, was almost at the end of his life.[176] Betjeman is satirizing the world that Symons lived in with his phraseology. Symons is lit by Modernist light and London remains a kind of fairyland (an image that certainly comes across in Symons' writing). He is confused by the offering of new ways of cooking both chicken and whitebait, suggesting by this analogy that the literary world emerging had altered remarkably, and that there was now no place for him. Betjeman seems to be observing the passing into oblivion of this kind of world that Symons was such a core part of; his ironic final sextet echoing a vision of a changed world, distant from decadence, but also laced with confusion and perhaps even madness:

> Where is Oscar? Where is Bosie?
> Have I seen that man before?
> And the old ones in the corner,
> Is it really Wratislaw?"
> Scent of Tutti-Frutti-Sen-Sen
> And cheroots upon the floor.[177]

Beckson and Munro contend that for the final twenty years of his life, Symons was very isolated as his "old friends died one by one" going "up to London occasionally visiting his old haunts" and it was clearly on one of these occasions that Betjeman witnessed him. Their contention is that Symons was very much now part of a "nearly forgotten past".[178] It may well have been Betjeman and his generation who mocked Symons' art and aesthetic, in so doing perhaps shovel-

---

luck, in a Letter to John Quinn, 13 October 1921, Symons asks "How can I pay for a dinner in the Café Royal?" The Café Royal is located on Regents Street. Rhoda's acting work had also dried up. See Letter to John Quinn, 13 October 1921, MS., Quinn. Cited in Beckson and Monro 2015.

176 Confirmed by Beckson and Munro 1989:203–4.

177 Betjeman 1990. Bosie was Lord Alfred Bruce Douglas (1870–1945), a British poet and journalist, best known as the lover of Oscar Wilde. The nickname had been given to Douglas by his mother. The Wratislaw that Betjeman mentions is most probably Theodore Wratislaw (1871–1933), a British poet and civil servant who was in Symons' and Wilde's circle. A cheroot is a filterless cylindrical cigar with both ends clipped during its manufacture.

178 Beckson and Munro 1989.

ling him out of focus in Anglo-Cornish literary history, and reasserting their centrality. The calling out for Oscar [Wilde] and Bosie (his lover) is particularly poignant. However, Betjeman possibly overstates the influence of Wilde on Symons. In fact, it was Dowson and individuals such as Walter Pater (1839–1894) who had more of a direct influence. Had Betjeman known better, he might well have been more sympathetic to Symons and what he had been trying to achieve. Had he known more of his Cornish credentials, a very different picture might have been offered, for in point of fact, Symons knew of Celticity in an equally rounded way as Betjeman articulated. Besides that, Symons had legitimate claim to Celtic ethnicity whereas Betjeman did not.

13

Conclusions:
Arthur Symons, Anglo-Cornish
Poet and Dramatist

At the height of his madness, in 1912 Symons wrote once more to the actress Julia Marlowe. As discussed above, Marlowe had been unable to help mount his play, *The Harvesters* in America, and Symons was still raw over that other failure: his Symbolist version of *Tristan and Iseult* and its once hoped-for production in Rome. In his letter, Symons is discussing actors with Marlowe, and his mind goes back to a point early on in his career when he helped Henry Irving to produce his editions of some of Shakespeare's best-known plays. We might expect Symons to note the ethnic link between them and he observes that "as I, he was Cornish" and this statement sees Symons wishing to convince Marlowe of his tenacity, but also perhaps his difference.[179]

What is most significant in his comments about Irving is that he notes that like Symons himself, Irving had what he terms, "that imagination".[180] The suggestion is that all Cornishmen and women have "that imagination" and that somehow imaginative proclivity was allied to this ethnicity.[181] It is a point well made, since over time, Cornwall has continued to produce not only a continuum of relevant and dynamic theatre, but also a set of novelists, poets, dramatists, and now film-makers who continue to deliver what Symons understood as "that imagination".

---

179 Letter to Julia Marlowe, 17 February 1912, MS., Museum, NY. Cited in Beckson and Monro 2015:321.

180 Letter to Julia Marlowe, 17 February 1912, MS., Museum, NY. Cited in Beckson and Monro 2015:321.

181 This is a point often articulated by Val Baker. See Val Baker 1972, 1982. It is a point attested in an alternative manner by Trower 2012, and Kent 2000.

For Symons this was something utterly non-English and it could not be found anywhere else in Europe. Whilst Symons is mainly considered as a founder of Symbolism and a key figure within the Decadent Movement, this volume has hopefully investigated a whole new side of Symons, which it is fair to say, now needs further academic treatment. Symons cannot be described as being prolific (indeed, the twenty years of his madness impacted massively on his output), and he had many other concerns aside from matters directly related to Cornwall and his Celticity. However, it still seems odd that whilst comparable figures such as Sir Arthur Quiller Couch are celebrated for their impact in Anglo-Cornish literature and letters (despite him having many other interests in other genres and fields), Arthur Symons is not much recognized. He was clearly a frustrated dramatist and the work that has survived gives us a tantalizing insight into a drama of the early twentieth-century which was both Symbolist in feel, and which dovetailed into the Decadent Movement. It is a pity that *The Minister's Call* has been lost and that his version of *Tristan and Iseult* was not more successful. At least the latter has not gone the way of the very earliest Tristan text, and has survived.

In Symons, we see the missing link to some of the great Anglo-Cornish dramas of the late nineteenth century, and those emerging as part of the Revivalist movement in Cornwall.[182] His Anglo-Cornish poetry was a bitter-sweet affair, effectively "all salt and honey", but it is one that had a profound influence on Yeats and which can be nearly inserted as the another missing part of the jigsaw found between the works of say John Harris and Robert Stephen Hawker, and the urgency of post-war poetry in Cornwall. He has always been there, but now can be better located as a voice in the midst of other key figures of this phase such as Thomas Hardy, James Dryden Hosken, Bernard Moore, Maud Cherill, Ruth Manning-Saunders, Anne Treneer and Hugh MacDiamid.[183] There are moments too, where his verse is comparable to that giant of Modernism in Cornwall and indeed "decadent" homosexuality in the form of A. L. Rowse.[184] That however, is a study for another time.

---

182 See Kent 2000:147–94.

183 For an overview, see Kent 2004.

184 See Payton 2005. There is a sense that Rowse kept his "decadence" secret from Cornwall because in his view it would never be tolerated there.

Symons further proves that in contrast to perceived wisdom and Anglo-centric literary criticism, in him we see an admirer of wider European Symbolism and decadence, actually at the heart of Anglo-Cornish ambitions and literary culture. Such European-wide figures in Cornish culture are not celebrated enough. Ironically, Symons knew precisely what he was trying to do: his choice of key historic narrative in the form of Tristan and Iseult instantly connects him to a Europe-wide literary masterpiece that only he had the audacity to re-tell during this phase. Somehow, despite dislocations in ethnicity and birthplace, Symons knew in its ancient symbolism and decadence that he was the perfect man for the job. He too, was the only figure who could wittily reposition a Celtic saint (good St Meriadoc) into a bloodthirsty revenger. The move was mad, decadent but brilliant.

ACKNOWLEDGEMENTS

I am indebted to the following individuals for their comments and observations on this volume: Peter Brooke, Brendan McMahon, Nicholas Williams, Julie Tamblin, and Andrew C. Symons. The University of Columbia and the British Library also responded swiftly and comprehensively to my requests.

14
Bibliography and References

NEWSPAPERS, MAGAZINES AND JOURNALS

Athenaeum
Bookman
Cornish Magazine
Cornish Telegraph
James Joyce Quarterly
Journal of the Royal Institution of Cornwall
London Quarterly Review
Savoy
Studies in English Literature
Tristania
Victorian Poetry

BOOKS, ARTICLES AND PAMPHLETS

Ackroyd, Peter. 1983. *The Last Testament of Oscar Wilde*. London: Hamish Hamilton.
Adams, Jad. 2001. *Madder Music, Stronger Wine: The Life of Ernest Dowson, Poet and Decadent*. London: Tauris Parke.
Anon. 1984. *Names for the Cornish*. Redruth: Dyllansow Truran.
Bawden, Nina. 2007. "Castle Dor" in Taylor, Helen (ed.). 2007, pp.192–6.
Beckson, Karl (ed.). 1977. *The Memoirs of Arthur Symons: Life and Art in the 1890s*. London: Pennsylvania State University Press.
——(ed.). 1981. *Aesthetes and Decadents of the 1890s: Anthology of British Poetry and Prose*. Chicago: Academy Chicago Publishers.
——. 1987. *Arthur Symons: A Life*. Oxford: Clarendon Press.
——. 1990. "The Tumbler of water and the cup of wine: Symons, Yeats and the Symbolist movement" in *Victorian Poetry*, Vol 28, No 3/4, Autumn-Winter, p.129.
Beckson, Karl and Munro, John M. 1970. "Symons, Browning and the development of the modern aesthetic" in *Studies in English Literature*, Autumn, pp. 687–699
——(eds.). 1989. *Arthur Symons: Selected Letters 1880–1935*, Iowa City: University of Iowa Press.
Bédier, Joseph. 1902–1905. *La Roman de Tristan*. Paris: Privately published.

BIBLIOGRAPHY AND REFERENCES

Belloc, Hilaire and Rosenfield, Paul (eds. and trs.). 1945. *Joseph Bédier: The Romance of Tristan*. New York: Vintage.

Belsey, Catherine. 1994. *Desire: Love Stories in Western Culture*. Oxford: Blackwell.

Betjeman, John. 1960. *Summoned by Bells*. London: John Murray.

———.1990. *Collected Poems*, London: John Murray.

Bizzotto, Elisa and Evangelista, Stefano (eds.). 2018. *Arthur Symons: Poet, Critic, Vagabond*. Oxford: Legenda.

Boland, Stephanie. 2017. "The 'Cornish tokens' of *Finnegan's Wake*: A journey through the Celtic archipelago" in *James Joyce Quarterly*, 54.1–2, 105–18.

Boyiopoulos, Kostas. 2015. *The Decadent Image: The Poetry of Wilde, Symons, and Dowson*. Edinburgh, Edinburgh University Press.

Boyiopoulos, Kostas, Patterson, Anthony and Sandy, Mark (eds). 2019. *Literary and Cultural Alternatives to Modernism: Unsettling Presences*. Abingdon: Routledge.

Brannigan, John. 1998. *New Historicism and Cultural Materialism*. Basingstoke: Palgrave Macmillan.

Burns, Marjorie J. 2005. *Perilous Realms: Celtic and Norse in Tolkien's Middle-Earth*. Toronto: University of Toronto Press.

Carruthers, Gerard and Rawe, Alan (eds.). 2003. *English Romanticism and the Celtic World*. Cambridge: Cambridge University Press.

Cave, Richard Allen (ed.). 1997. *W. B. Yeats: Selected Plays*, London: Penguin.

———(ed.). 2000. *Oscar Wilde: The Importance of Being Earnest and Other Plays*. London: Penguin.

Chisholm, Hugh (ed.). 1911. "Nisard, Jean Marie Napoleon Désiré" in *Encyclopædia Britannica*, 19 (11th ed.), Cambridge: Cambridge University Press, p.709

Chubb, Ray (ed. and tr.). 2018. *Bewnans Meriasek: The Camborne Play*, Portreath: Agan Tavas.

Clark, Carol (ed. and tr.). 2004. *Charles-Pierre Baudalaire: Selected Poems*. London: Penguin.

Clemo, Jack. 1975 [1949]. *Confession of a Rebel*. London: Chatto and Windus.

Clunie, Grace and Maginess, Tess. 2015. *The Celtic Spirit in Literature*. Dublin: The Columba Press.

Combellack, Myrna, *The Camborne Play: A Verse Translation*. Redruth: Dyllansow Truran.

Creasey, Matthew (ed.). 2014. *Arthur Symons: Symbolist Movement in Literature*, 1899, rev. 1919, Manchester: Carcenet.

de Mandach, André. 1979. "Legend and Reality: Recent Excavation and Research in Cornwall concerning Tristan and Isolt" in *Tristania*, Vol.IV, No.2.

Ditmus, E. M. R. 1979. *Tristan and Iseult in Cornwall*. Brockworth: Forrester Roberts.

Doble, Gilbert H. 1997. The Saints *of Cornwall: Part One – Saints of the Land's End District [1923–1944]*. Felinfach: Llanerch

Dorn, Karen. 1983. *Players and Painted Stage: Theatre of W. B. Yeats*. Totowa, New Jersey: Harvester Wheatsheaf.

Dowson, Ernest. 1905. *The Poems*. Portland: Thomas B. Mosher.

———. 2017. *The Poems and Prose*, CreateSpace Independent Publishing Platform, 2017

Duncker, Patricia and Constantine, Helen (eds. and trs.). 2005. *Théophile Gautier: Mademoiselle de Maupin [1835]*. London: Penguin.

Ellis, Peter Berresford. 1974. *The Cornish Language and its Literature*. London and New York: Routledge and Kegan Paul.

——.1988 [1985]. *The Celtic Revolution: A Study in Anti-Imperialism*. Talybont: Y Lolfa.

——.1993. *The Celtic Dawn: A History of Pan-Celticism*. London: Constable.

Fredrick, Alan S. (ed. and tr.). 1970. *Béroul: The Romance of Tristan*. Harmondsworth: Penguin.

Frayne John P and Johnson, Colton (eds.). 1975. *Uncollected Prose by W. B. Yeats, Vol 2, Reviews, Articles and Miscellaneous Prose, 1897–1939*. Basingstoke, MacMillan.

Grigg, Erik. 2008. *Beunans Meriasek [The Life of St, Meriasek]: A Study Guide*. Cornwall: The Cornish Language Board.

Grimbert, Joan Tasker (ed.) 1995. *Tristan and Isolde: A Casebook*. New York and London: Garland.

Hampton, Christopher. 1990. *The Ideology of the Text*. Milton Keynes: Open University Press.

Hardie, Melissa (ed.), 1992. *A Mere Interlude: Some Literary Visitors to Lyonesse*. Newmill: The Pattern Press.

Hardy, Thomas. 1923. *The Famous Tragedy of the Queen of Cornwall at Tintagel in Lyonesse*. London: Macmillan.

Harris, Markham (ed. and tr.). 1977. *The Life of Meriasek: A Medieval Cornish Miracle Play*. Washington D.C.: Catholic University of America Press.

Harrison, Anthony M. 1995. "Swinburne's Tristram of Lyonesse: Visionary and Courtly Epic" in Grimbert, Joan Tasker (ed.) 1995, pp.301–24.

Hatto. A. T. (ed. and tr.).1967. *Gottfried von Strassburg: Tristan, with the Tristan of Thomas*. Harmondsworth: Penguin.

Hayes, Sebastian. 2007. *Arthur Symons: Leading Poet of the English Decadence*. On-line: Brimstone Press.

Hechter, Michael. 1975. *Internal Colonialism: The Celtic Fringe in British National Development, 1536–1966*. London: Routledge and Kegan Paul.

Hext, Kate and Murray, Alex (eds.). 2019. *Decadence in the Age of Modernism*, Baltimore. Maryland: John Hopkins University Press.

Holdsworth, Roger (ed.). 2003. *Arthur Symons: Selected Writing*. New York: Routledge.

Howes, Marjorie (ed.). 2006. *The Cambridge Companion to W. B. Yeats*. Cambridge: Cambridge University Press.

Hunt, Robert. 1865. *Popular Romances of the West of England: The Drolls: Traditions, and Superstitions of Old Cornwall (Second Series)*. London: John Camden Hotten.

Hurst, John. 1993. "Literature in Cornwall" in Payton, Philip (ed.) 1993, pp.291–308

Irving, Henry. 1898. "Sir Henry Irving's Childhood: The Great Actor's Reminiscences of Cornwall" in Quiller-Couch, Arthur (ed.). 1898. *The Cornish Magazine*, Vol. 1, Truro: Joseph Pollard, pp.105–10

Jefferies, Norman (ed.). 1990. *W. B. Yeats: Selected Poetry*. London: Macmillan.

Jenner, Henry. n.d. "Cornwall: A Celtic Nation" in Williams. Derek R. (ed.). 2004:56–69.

BIBLIOGRAPHY AND REFERENCES

——. 1914. "The Tristan Romance and its Cornish Provenance" in *Journal of the Royal Institution of Cornwall*. No.14, pp. 464–88.

——. 2010 [1904]. *Henry Jenner: Handbook of the Cornish Language*. Second edition. Edited by Michael Everson. Cathair na Mart: Evertype, 2010.

Jensen, Robert. 1994. *Marketing Modernism in Fin-de-Siècle Europe*. Princeton: Princeton University Press.

Jones, Kelvin L. 2019. *The Lewisham Poet: The Life and Works of Ernest Dowson*. Surrey: Kelvin L. Jones.

Joyce, James. 1992 [1939]. *Finnegan's Wake*. London: Penguin.

Kent, Alan M. 2000. *The Literature of Cornwall: Continuity, Identity, Difference 1000–2000*. Bristol: Redcliffe.

——(ed.). 2000. *Voices from West Barbary: An Anthology of Anglo-Cornish Poetry 1549–1928*. London: Francis Boutle Publishers.

——. 2002. *Pulp Methodism: The Lives and Literature of Silas, Joseph and Salome Hocking*. St Austell: Cornish Hillside Publications.

——. 2004. "Song of our Motherland: Making Meaning of the Life and Work of Katharine Lee Jenner" in Williams, Derek R. (ed.) 2004:119–57

——. 2005. "Scatting it t'lerrups: Provisional Notes towards Alternative Methodologies in Language and Literary Studies in Cornwall" in Philip Payton (ed.) 2005:23–52

——. 2010. *The Hope of Place: Selected Poems*, London: Francis Boutle Publishers.

——. 2019. *Turning Serpentine*. Wellington: Halsgrove.

Kerman, Joseph. 1995. "Wagner's *Tristan and Isolde*: Opera as Symphonic Poem" in Grimbert, Joan Tasker (ed.). 1995, pp.35–76.

Kerrigan, John. 2008. *Archipelagic English: Literature, History and Politics 1602–1707*. Oxford: Oxford University Press.

Kittow, Sue. 2015. *Walks in the Footsteps of Cornish Writers*. Wilmslow: Sigma Press.

Kneehigh Theatre. 2005. *Tristan and Iseult, The Bacchae, The Wooden Frock, The Red Shoes*. London: Oberon Books.

Koch, John T. and John Carey, John (eds.). 1995. *The Celtic Heroic Age: Literary Sources for Ancient Celtic Europe and Early Ireland and Wales*. Malden, Massachusetts: Celtic Studies Publications.

Loth, Joseph. 1892. *De Nouvelles Théories sur l'origine du Roman Arthurien*. Paris: Privately published.

Maclean, John. 1873. *The parochial and family history of the deanery of Trigg Minor, in the county of Cornwall*. Vol. II. Bodmin: Liddel and Son.

March, Caeia. 1993. *Reflections*. London: The Women's Press.

McGuinness, Patrick and Baldick, Robert (eds. and trs.). 2003. *Joris-Karl Huysman: Against Nature [1884]*. London: Penguin.

Mighall, Robert (ed.). 2003. *Oscar Wilde: The Picture of Dorian Gray*. London: Penguin.

Muddiman, Bernard. 1921. *The Men of the Nineties*. New York: G.P. Putnam's Sons.

Muret, Ernest (ed.). 1903. *Le Roman de Tristan par Béroul*. Paris: Firmin Didot et Compagnie.

Munro, John M. 1969. *Arthur Symons*. New York: Twayne Publishers.

Ó Cróinín, Dáibhí. 2009. *Whitley Stokes (1830–1909): The Lost Celtic Notebooks Rediscovered*, Dublin: Four Courts Press.

Owens, W. R. and Johnson, Hamish (eds.). 1998. *Romantic Writings: An Anthology*. Milton Keynes: The Open University.

Patten, Bernard M. 2020. *The Search of Tristan and Iseult: A Postmodern Metafictional Travel Romance*. Amazon: Kindle.

Payton, Philip (ed.). 1993. *Cornwall Since War: The Contemporary History of a European Region*. Redruth: Institute of Cornish Studies and Dyllansow Truran.

——(ed.) 2005. *Cornish Studies: Thirteen*. Exeter: University of Exeter Press.

——. 2005. *A. L. Rowse and Cornwall: A Paradoxical Patriot*. Exeter: University of Exeter Press.

——. 2010. *John Betjeman and Cornwall: "The Celebrated Cornish Nationalist"*. Exeter: University of Exeter Press.

Phelps, Kenneth. 1975. *The Wormwood Cup – Thomas Hardy in Cornwall: A study in Temperament, Topography and Timing*. Padstow: Lodenek Press.

Phelpstead, Carl. 2011. *Tolkien and Wales: Language, Literature and Identity*. Cardiff: University of Wales Press.

Phillips, K. C. 1993. *Roche Rhymes*. Padstow: Tabb House.

Poulson, Christine. 1995. "'That Most Beautiful of Dreams': Tristram and Isoud in British Art of the Nineteenth and Early Twentieth Centuries" in Grimbert, Joan Tasker (ed.). 1995, pp.325–56.

——. 1999. *The Quest for the Grail: Arthurian Legend in British Art 1840–1920*. Manchester: Manchester University Press.

Quiller-Couch, Arthur (ed.). 1898. *The Cornish Magazine*, Vol. 1, Truro: Joseph Pollard

Quiller-Couch, Arthur and du Maurier, Daphne. 1962. *Castle Dor*. London: Dent.

Robbins, Catherine Ruth. 1996. *Decadence and sexual politics in three Fin-de-Siecle Writers: Oscar Wilde, Arthur Symons and Vernon Lee*. Warwick: University of Warwick Press.

Roberts, Forrester. 1998. *The Legend of Tristan and Iseult: The Tale and the Trail in Ireland, Cornwall and Brittany*. Gloucester: Forrester Roberts.

Rodensky, Lisa (ed.). 2006. *Decadent Poetry from Wilde to Naidu*, London: Penguin.

Shackleton, Robert. 1961. *Montesquieu: A Critical Biography*. London: Oxford University Press.

Shaw, Michael. 2019. *The Fin-De-Siecle Scottish Revival: Romance, Decadence and Celtic Identity*. Edinburgh: Edinburgh University Press.

Shaw, Thomas. 1962. *Saint Petroc and John Wesley, Apostles in Cornwall: An Examination of the Celtic Background of Cornish Methodism*. Cornwall: Cornish Methodist Historical Association.

——.1967. *A History of Cornish Methodism*. Truro: D. Bradford Barton

Sinfield, Alan. 1992. *Faultlines: Cultural Materialism and the Politics of Dissident Reading*. Oxford: Clarendon Press.

Smith, A. S. D. 1951. *Trystan hag Isolt*. Redruth: J and M. Roberts.

Stokes, Whitley (ed. and tr.). 1872. *The Life of Saint Meriasek, Bishop and Confessor: A Cornish Drama*. London: Trübner and Co.

Sutcliff, Rosemary. 1971. *Tristan and Iseult*. London: The Bodley Head.

BIBLIOGRAPHY AND REFERENCES

Swinburne, A. C. 1899. *Tristram of Lyonesse and Other Poems*. London: Chatto and Windus.

Symons, Arthur. 1886. *An Introduction to the Study of Browning*. London; Cassell and Co.

——. 1889. *Days and Nights*. London: Macmillan Co.

——. 1892. *Silhouettes*. Mathews and Lane.

——.1896. *London Nights*. L. C. Smithers.

——. 1896. "A Causerie: From a castle in Ireland" in *The Savoy*, 6, October, p.95

——. 1897. *Amoris Victima*. L. C. Smithers.

——.1948 [1898]. *Aubrey Beardsley*. London: At the Sign of the Unicorn.

——(tr.). 1898. *Gabriele D'Annunzio: The Child of Pleasure*. London: W. Heinemann.

——.1899. *Images of Good and Evil*. London: W. Heinemann.

——(tr.). 1900. *Gabriele D'Annunzio: The Dead City*, London: W. Heinemann.

——. 1902. *Poems*. London: W. Heinemann.

——. 1903. "Review of W. B. Yeats' *Ideas of Good and Evil*" in the *Athenaeum*, 27 June.

——. 1905. *The Fool of the World and Other Poems*, London, W. Heinemann.

——. 1909. *The Romantic Movement in English Poetry*. London: Archibald Constable and Co.

——(tr.). 1915. *Émile Verhaeren: The Dawn*. London: Duckworth and Co.

——. 1917. *Tristan and Iseult: A Play in Four Acts*. London: William Heinemann.

——. 1917. *Tristan and Iseult: A Play in Four Acts*. New York: Brentano's.

——. 1919. *The Toy Cart*. London: Maunsel and Co.

——. 2019 [1921] *Spiritual Adventures*. London: Forgotten Books.

——. 1930. *Confessions: A Study in Pathology*. New York: Fountain Press.

Synge, J. M. 2009 [1912]. *Travels in Wicklow, West Kerry and Connemara*. London: Serif.

——.1961 [1907] *The Aran Islands*. London: George Allen and Unwin.

Taylor, Helen (ed.). 2007. *The Daphne du Maurier Companion*. London: Virago.

Thomas, Charles. 1967. *Christian Antiquities of Camborne*. St Austell: H. E. Warne.

Thomas, D. M. 1983. *Selected Poems*. Harmondsworth: Penguin.

Thompson, Luke. 2016. *Clay Phoenix: A Biography of Jack Clemo*. London: Ally.

Trower, Shelley. 2012. *Rocks of Nation: The Imagination of Celtic Cornwall*. Manchester: University of Manchester Press.

Val Baker, Denys. 1972. *The Timeless Land: The Creative Spirit in Cornwall*, Bath: Adams and Dart

——.1982. *A View from Land's End: Writers Against a Cornish Background*. London: William Kimber.

Watkins, D. H. 1962. *Trystan hag Isolt*. Camborne: An Lef Kernewek.

Williams, Derek R. (ed.). 2004. *Henry and Katharine Jenner: A Celebration of Cornwall's Culture, language and Identity*. London: Francis Boutle Publishers.

Williams, J. E. Caerwyn (ed.). 1971. *Literature in the Celtic Countries*. Cardiff: University of Wales Press.

Williams, Mark. 2016. *Irish Immortals: A History of the Gods of Irish Myth*. Princeton: Princeton University Press.

Wolff, Janet. 1993. *The Social Production of Art*, Basingstoke: Macmillan.

Wyatt, Stephen (ed.). 1985. *Pinero: Three Plays – The Magistrate, The Second Mrs Tanqueray and Trelawny of the Wells*. London: Methuen.

AUDIO-VISUAL RESOURCE

Reynolds, Kevin (dir.). 2006. *Tristan and Isolde*, Los Angeles: 20th Century Fox.

INTERNET RESOURCES

Maclean, John. 1876. *The Parochial and Family History of the Deanery of Trigg Minor. in the Country of Cornwall*. Vol. II. https://archive.org/stream /cu31924081264826 accessed 2021-07-22.

Malory Thomas. *Le Morte D'Arthur*. Illustrated by Abrey Beardsley. https:// web.archive.org/web/20210114110621/https://enchantedbooklet.com/le -morte-darthur/ accessed 2021-07-22.

Queer Lorgnette. "Invisible Lesbians (Opera Edition)". https://web.archive.org/web /20210820174516/https://qlorgnette.wordpress.com/2020/04/25/invisible -lesbians-opera-edition accessed 2021-08-22.

Symons, Arthur, & Aubrey Beardsley. 1896. *The Savoy*. https://archive.org/details /savoy01symo accessed 2021-07-22.

Verse in *Tristan and Iseult*

In typesetting this book I had occasion to examine both the Heinemann and Brentano editions. I think the Heinemann is the more attractive of the two, and I have favoured some of its typographic conventions, mainly the use of SMALL CAPS and casing in character names.

Tristan and Iseult is a play written in iambic pentameter, with lines having 10 or 11 syllables. In many instances a line is divided between two speakers, but neither of the 1917 editions took this into account and each part of each broken line was typeset flush left. In this edition I have made use of dropped lines in the usual fashion, and I have added line numbers to indicate the line count.

There was no need to count the syllables in each line, but some observations can be made. Consider line III.271:

MELOT, *as he goes.*
I have cracked the nut; they will scramble for the pieces.

Ordinarily one might think the would require "I've" and "they'll" to make the syllable count right. And so they should—but here the poet has expanded the abbreviations for a kind of staccato emphasis from Melot, as he goes. Or so it seems to me.

The ten deliberately short lines in the text make me wonder about the poet's intention. The most interesting to me is what I call an echo. In the 1917 editions, line I.263 was printed as two short lines beginning with capital letters; these look like short lines, but are not:

KING OF IRELAND.
I am well content   263a
To hold him for ally.   263b

Since those two lines make a single metric line, I think it's a 1917 typesetting error and I have amended it:

KING OF IRELAND.
I am well content to hold him for ally.   263
QUEEN.   More than ally.   264

Part of the reason for this is line I.264, with only four syllables—but those echo the end of the previous line (and I have indented it accordingly). This echo takes them outside the metrical scheme for a moment. Line II.72 is similar, though it is only a syllabic echo:

ISEULT OF IRELAND.   Go.   70
Sleep, rest, and come again.
        [BRANGAENE *goes out.* ISEULT *sits in meditation. There is a*
        pause, and TRISTAN *enters.*]
TRISTAN.   You sent for me.   71
ISEULT OF IRELAND.   How is this, sir?   72

Line III.91 is likewise an echo

ISEULT OF IRELAND.
If death should come upon us in this hour,   89
What would you say? Would you thank God for life?   90
TRISTAN.   I would thank God for life,   91

And in line IV.280 we have yet another, echoing the last voice in the previous broken line:

TRISTAN.
Look straight.
ISEULT OF BRITTANY.
                I see, I see.
TRISTAN.   Is the sail white?   279
ISEULT OF BRITTANY, *slowly turning her eyes at* TRISTAN.
                          The sail is black.   280

Some of the short lines are just for interjections of various kinds: III.197 "Coward to me!", III.318 "Kill Mark!", IV.124 "Oh no, oh no.". In Act III there are two linked short lines:

ISEULT OF IRELAND.
Tristan, it is my life   131
[…]
TRISTAN, *drawing back from her and looking to her eyes.*
Iseult, there is an end,   139

Not long after this in the same scene we have III.164 "Love is not love", a line with a certain intensity. Are all three linked? *It is my life… there is an end… love is not love…*

Symons' verse was competent and well suited to the work. It's interesting to see patterns in his verse when he deviates from the main metre of the play.

Michael Everson
Dundee, November 2021

Tristan and Iseult: A Play in Four Acts

TO
ELEONORA DUSE.
Non sentite il sangue delle rose stillare
Tra le mie dita nelle vostre dux mani?

TRISTANO E ISOTTA, *Atto III*

THE PERSONS.

KING MARK OF CORNWALL.

THE KING OF IRELAND.

TRISTAN: *Nephew of King Mark of Cornwall.*

MERIADOC: *Nephew of the Queen of Ireland.*

MELOT: *A Fool at the court of King Mark.*

A PHYSICIAN.

THE QUEEN OF IRELAND.

ISEULT OF IRELAND: *Daughter of the Queen.*

ISEULT OF BRITTANY: *Cousin of Iseult of Ireland.*

BRANGAENE: *A lady in attendance on Iseult of Ireland.*

YGRAINE

ELAINE   } *Ladies in attendance on Iseult of Brittany.*

IMOGEN

A CHILD.

LORDS AND ATTENDANTS.

The action takes place Ireland, Cornwall, Brittany, and on the sea.

ACT I.

The scene represents a large room in the palace of the KING OF IRELAND. *There are vacant seats in the foreground on the right. In the background are two long broad steps leading to an inner room, which is seen as through the proscenium of a theatre. Women are seated just inside, working at embroidery frames. In the front is* ISEULT OF BRITTANY, *working; behind her is* BRANGAENE. ISEULT OF IRELAND *is standing beside her, looking at the work. As the curtain goes up, a large door on the left is opened, and the* QUEEN *enters.* MERIADOC *following her as if in eager conversation. They cross to the seats and sit down.* ISEULT OF IRELAND *comes down the steps and across the stage, with an eager movement.*

ISEULT OF IRELAND.
Mother, I knew that Tristan would come back.

QUEEN.
Why not? These wandering children of the harp
Follow the crying people of the air;
They know their seasons, they return with them.
Tristan will bring his harp into the hall   5
When he has rested. And now, Meriadoc,
Speak on.

MERIADOC.
      I say again, the time has come.
It is a year now since my father died;
He was your brother, you have loved him well,
Almost as I have loved him, and I have loved   10
Your daughter and my father and no more.

ISEULT OF IRELAND.
Why do you speak of me?
    [*She sits down, looking away from him.*]

MERIADOC.   I have said the word,
Which must return to silence. Be it so.
I speak another thing now. I desire
Vengeance for Morolt, blood for Morolt's blood.   15

QUEEN.
And I desire no less, yet, Meriadoc,
Since no man knows the spiller of that blood,
Vengeance but an arm that smites a sword
Into the empty, dark, and yielding air.

MERIADOC.
Give me but leave, and I will find the man.   20

QUEEN.
I will both give you leave, and give you that
Which when you find him shall find out his life
Surer than any hound. Here, take the key,
Iseult, and bring me the knife, bring it with care,
You know its secret.

ISEULT OF IRELAND.
             I will bring it, mother.   25
    [*She goes back to the inner room, unlocks an oak chest which
    stands against the side wall, and takes out a sheathed dagger.*]
(*To* ISEULT OF BRITTANY)
What would you do with such a cruel thing?
Kind cousin Iseult?

ISEULT OF BRITTANY.
             Cast it in the sea,
My manly hearted cousin.

ISEULT OF IRELAND, *holding it up.*
                    Is it not strange
That men play such forbidden games with death,
And we too deal the pieces? This rare thing   30
Will find the heart some woman's heart shall break for.

ISEULT OF BRITTANY.
Why do you take it in your hands?

ISEULT OF IRELAND.   I? Merely
To take it to my mother.
        [*She carries it across to her mother, who takes it, turns it over,*
        and as she speaks gives it to MERIADOC.]

QUEEN.   This knife I give you
Has lapped up poison night by night, and slept
Under the moon, and I have watched him sleep.   35
I give the knife to you: use it but once.
        [MERIADOC *takes the knife and holds out the cross-shaped hilt.*]

MERIADOC.
I swear upon this cross to use the knife
Once, and no more. Cousin, before I go—

ISEULT OF IRELAND.
Cousin, no more of that.

MERIADOC.   You take me ill.
It is another thing I have to ask.   40

ISEULT OF IRELAND.
Where do you go?

MERIADOC.   To Cornwall.

ISEULT OF IRELAND.   A stern land.
You know not whom you seek; why do you go?

MERIADOC.
Give me a thing you keep.

ISEULT OF IRELAND.   What shall I give you?

MERIADOC.
The splinter of the sword that killed my father.
Give it to me, and it shall draw the sword   45
Out of the deadly iron of the earth
Like a strong loadstone; it will know its sword.

ISEULT OF IRELAND, *after a pause.*
Yes, I will give it to you, Meriadoc.
> [*She rises and moves slowly across the stage towards the chest,
> which she had left open. The door is thrown open and an*
> ATTENDANT *enters.*]

ATTENDANT.
Lord Tristan.
> [TRISTAN *enters and walks slowly towards the* QUEEN.
> ISEULT *pauses and half turns, with her hand on the lid of the
> chest, looking fiercely at* TRISTAN.]

QUEEN.   In the name of both our lands,
Welcome. A year seems but a day and night,   50
And I some easy sleeper, since we heard
The voices of your harp among our own.

TRISTAN.
Madam, the heaped good wishes of a year,
Longer in absence than its counted days,
Crowd back each other, asking to be first.   55
> [*He turns towards* ISEULT, *who has slowly approached.*]
Princess, I buy my welcome at our hands
With songs that I have made for you to sing;
You loved them once.

ISEULT OF IRELAND.   I am your pupil still.
[*She goes towards* MERIADOC *as if unconscious of her intention.*]

MERIADOC.
Iseult! the gift!

ISEULT OF IRELAND.
                    What was it? I forget.
[*She stands gazing at* TRISTAN *in silence.*]

QUEEN.
Was the sea fair in coming?

TRISTAN.   Fair and fierce.   60

ISEULT OF IRELAND.
The sea is friends with you.

TRISTAN.   I follow it:
I have no other will than the sea's will.

QUEEN.
My daughter, sit beside me. You, my lord.
Here.
ISEULT OF IRELAND.
        I must have Iseult of the White Hands.
Come, cousin, leave the armour of the knight: 65
It is but wool upon a frame; but here
Is the true knight; come down and welcome him.

        [ISEULT OF BRITTANY *rises slowly, lays down the wool on her
        embroidery frame, comes slowly across the stage. The others fol-
        low her.* TRISTAN *rises and bows low.*]

TRISTAN.
I have called off your fingers from some dream
That you were weaving.

ISEULT OF BRITTANY.   I was only weaving
A knight in armour, dying; there in grass,   70
An apple orchard, birds singing, and sheep.

ISEULT OF IRELAND.
Have you not such a story in your songs?
But not as fair a lady in your land
As this that bears my name!

TRISTAN.   Few quite so fair
For she is fair, yet not as Helen was,   75
Not as you are.

ISEULT OF IRELAND.
         What is Helen, sir, to me?
But this white cousin Iseult of my name,
Read me this woman, Tristan; read her soul;
Look in her eyes and tell me what she is.

ISEULT OF BRITTANY.
I pray you do not tell me what you see.   80

TRISTAN.
She has the face of one who is content,
Making a little last with loving it.

ISEULT OF IRELAND.
In patience, then, the nurse of love? God keep
Such as are patient!

TRISTAN.   I have read as well
How earth was crumbled up for Helen's sake   85
And cast like crumbs to birds.

ISEULT OF IRELAND.   Is love so cruel?
Is it not only in the song?

QUEEN.   My daughter,
Love is more cruel than a savage beast;
Therefore fear love.

ISEULT OF IRELAND.
              Why, how should the free soul
Fear any power under the firmament?   90
For there are women who have never feared
The face of steel or face any man
Or blood or battle or the foam of the sea
When the wind wrings out the sails and washes them.

TRISTAN.
It is such women that Love leaves to rule.   95

ISEULT OF IRELAND.
How should he rule them? they that do not weave
A dying knight in an orchard, but they can die.

TRISTAN.
Yes, die for love: a woman can do that.

ISEULT OF IRELAND.
O, any woman! more than die for love.
Tristan, I had an uncle whom I loved   100
More than I ever shall love man; this brave,
This tender, more than father to me, this
Glory of Ireland, was most fully slain.
        [She starts to her feet.]
If Morolt's murderer stood before me now
As you stand there, I, woman that I am,   105
(Give me your sword: I do not feat to see
The nakedness of steel: give it to my hand)
      [She takes TRISTAN's *sword from him and lifts it in the air.]*
I would dare—
      [She looks fixedly at the sword in her hand.]
         O, this is some witchcraft. No.

The sword, the sword, it cannot be the sword!
> [*She runs to the open chest, takes out the splinter, and fits it to the notch in the sword.*]

The sword is whole again. This sacred blood   110
Make my arm strong that I may drink his blood!
Die Tristan!
> [*She comes towards* TRISTAN *with the sword in her hand. All rise.* MERIADOC *puts his hand on his dagger. The* QUEEN *comes forward.*]

ISEULT OF BRITTANY, *catching* ISEULT OF IRELAND *and drawing her back.*
             Iseult, will you murder him?
If you are mad, kill me!

QUEEN.   Is it not madness?

TRISTAN.
Strike! I am at your mercy.

QUEEN.   Stay, Iseult!

ISEULT OF IRELAND.
Mother, look well upon the sword. See now,   115
Here is the splinter of the sword that killed
Morolt; see how they grow together; see
The sword that Morolt died by.

QUEEN.   We have been fooled,
We have given our enemy life.

MERIADOC, *drawing his dagger.*   You gave him life
That death might find him here.

ISEULT OF BRITTANY.   No, Meriadoc.   120

ISEULT OF IRELAND.
What is it to you, Iseult of Brittany
If this man live or die? No, Meriadoc,
My hand!

TRISTAN.
          Iseult of Ireland, why do you wait?
Your eyes have stabbed me: finish! you have the sword.   125

QUEEN.
Daughter, put down the sword, his is our guest.

ISEULT OF IRELAND.
He has our blood upon him.

QUEEN.   He has broken
Our bread. Put down the sword. Tristan, your life
I give you; get you gone out of our gates.
No, stand aside; be silent. All of you   130
Stand further off and leave us two alone.
     [TRISTAN *moves across the stage and stands alone.* MERIADOC
     stands apart on the other side, eyeing him. The others go out
     hastily. BRANGAENE *lingers by the door.*]

ISEULT OF BRITTANY, *as she crosses the stage, half-supported by*
  BRANGAENE.
What will the do to him? Save him for my sake,
Brangaene!

BRANGAENE.
          I do not need to; he is saved.

ISEULT OF IRELAND.
What shall we do, mother? Oh, mother, tell me
Why could I not kill Tristan? I had the will,   135
And it was not your hand that stayed my hand.

QUEEN.
Fate holds the hands of all men in the dark,
And there shall not a drop of blood be shed
Before its time, although we snatch up swords.

ISEULT OF IRELAND.
Mother, I hate him! he has spilt our blood.   140
Why is that my eyes follow his eyes,
As a hound follows his master?

QUEEN.   Do not ask:
There is no herb against the eyes of a man,
There is no stone shall turn his eyes aside.

ISEULT OF IRELAND.
Mother, must we forgive our enemy   145
And send his feet out of our house alive?

QUEEN.
He is our guest; we may not do him harm.
Daughter, if I, that so loved Morolt—blood
Could not wash out the tears I shed for him—
Can, for the honour of our house, forgive   150
Tristan, who slew him, can you not forgive?
I do not pardon him for pity, no,
But for my troth and honour.

ISEULT OF IRELAND.   Alas, mother,
That ever I was born to see this day!

MERIADOC, *coming up.*
O Queen, the knife is ready for his throat;   155
Say the word, and we are all at peace.

QUEEN.
It may not be; but yet I know not well
What must be, in this backward drift of things.
        [*While she is speaking,* BRANGAENE *comes forward.*]

BRANGAENE.
O mistress, let me speak. These things now past
Are over; but what shall be, that is ours.   160
Is not the honour of the Queen more worth
Than many lives? Let the Queen's honour live.
As for this knight, the kinsman of the King,
It may be he has come, not without cause,
But for your profit in all honour. Wait,   165
Speak gently to him, ask him why he came,
At peril of his life, back to these shores.

QUEEN.
This is well thought, Brangaene.

ISEULT OF IRELAND.   He has come
To bring into our midst some kind of death.
I know that if he goes out of our house   170
Living, we shall not all live well or long.
How can I hate him?

QUEEN.   Summon him, Brangaene.
        [TRISTAN *comes nearer.*]

TRISTAN.
Madam, I see my pardon in your eyes.
I have one word to say, and then I am silent
And wait your mercy. I have brought on you   175
Sorrow, yet of necessity. The sword
Of Morolt and my sword were in God's hands;
We fought a just and equal fight, and each
Fought for his life in peril of his death.

QUEEN.
Tristan, I pardon you, not willingly,   180
But for my honour, being here my guest
And sacred to my hearth. Here is my hand.
Iseult, your hand.

ISEULT OF IRELAND.
                Alas, that I must take
My enemy's hand in mine!
   [*She gives him her hand.*]

TRISTAN, *kissing the hand of the* QUEEN.
                    Queen, you have given
My life to me twice over, and I have   185
To serve you twofold now.
(*To* ISEULT)   Princess, I hold
My faith with you from this forth.

QUEEN.   Why did you come,
Knowing that you are fatal to our house?

TRISTAN.
May I speak out?

QUEEN.   Speak quickly.

TRISTAN.   If I may speak
Freely a king's speech, and being otherwise   190
The enemy of a king, I will disclose
The reason of my coming, which did but wait
No more than time for telling.

QUEEN.   If you have
A friendly approach, then speak it as to friends.

TRISTAN.
I am sent hither by King Mark of Cornwall,   195
My uncle, king of an unconquered realm,
Because he knew that his best enemy, Ireland,
Held the white pearl of the sea, and he desired
To wed the fairest woman in the world.

QUEEN.
Is this your word or his?

TRISTAN.   It is his word.   200
I am his speech-bearer, and in his name
I am to ask your daughter's hand for Mark.

ISEULT OF IRELAND.
Who praised me to King Mark?

TRISTAN.   Not least of others,
I.

ISEULT OF IRELAND.
   Then it was a lying tongue that spoke
A coward's praise.

QUEEN.   Daughter, there is no queen   205
Who would need wooing more than to be told
That Mark, the King of Cornwall, sought her hand.

ISEULT OF IRELAND.
Mother, you do wrong to women. I have known
A woman who would have had gladlier
A shepherd's apple from a shepherd's hand   210
Than crowns from shaking fingers.

QUEEN.   This is not
For you or me, but for the King your father.
The safety of our land may hang upon it.
We must have counsel and the voice of the King.
Sir, we give you instant hearing. Send,   215
Brangaene, quickly, to my lord the King
And crave the King's good pleasure.

BRANGAENE.   In haste, madam.
   [*She goes to the door and sends messengers.*]

QUEEN.
Sir, this must be lightly thought upon
Or idly spoken of. Weigh now your words
And tell me: is your king ready for peace?   220
His galleys have not often come our way
With less of spears than oars.

TRISTAN.   The King desires
Peace and the marriage of two hands in one.

QUEEN.
We also desire peace; but for this marriage—

ISEULT OF IRELAND.
May Iseult speak?

QUEEN.   Speak, Iseult.

ISEULT OF IRELAND.   There is no king,   225
Could give me greatness enough to fill up
The lack that he would make in me.

QUEEN.   What luck?
     [BRANGAENE *comes back.*]

ISEULT OF IRELAND.
Why, nothing but the lack of my own self;
I would rather be myself than be a queen.   230

BRANGAENE.
To be a queen is to have all the world
Instead of dreaming. If you had the world,
What would you do with it?

ISEULT OF IRELAND.   What, you too, Brangaene?

QUEEN.
Brangaene, summon those who were in the hall.
[*She goes out.*]

MERIADOC.
Cousin, you should have given me the sword!   235

ISEULT OF IRELAND.
The sword is old now, and it cannot stir,
And we must wait.
[*The guests re-enter, anxiously.*]

ISEULT OF BRITTANY.
                    What have they done to him?
He is living yet and smiles: I saw him dead.
She talks apart, patient and angry.

ANOTHER WOMAN, *aside.*   See,
The Queen looks hard at Tristan, watching him   240
With some new purpose.

ANOTHER WOMAN.   Hush! here is the King.
[*The* KING *comes in and goes up to the* QUEEN.

QUEEN.
My lord, a boon. I ask a boon that lies
Neat to my heart and to your daughter's heart.

KING OF IRELAND.
Is not the thing you ask already yours?
You are not so glad to ask as I to give.   245
What is the boon?

QUEEN.   My lord, to pardon Tristan.
He stands before you; I am surety for him,
He killed my brother Morolt: pardon him.

KING OF IRELAND.
This is the strangest boon was ever asked.
Was Morolt not your brother? Yet, so be it.   250
If you have pardoned Tristan, so have I.
Here is my hand, sir.

TRISTAN, *kneeling and kissing his hand.*
                              Grave, my lord the King,
Grace for my lord and master.

KING OF IRELAND.   Be it so
For you, since the Queen wills it, and for him
In his own honour. Rise and sit with me.   255

QUEEN.
My lord, this grave and most unlooked-for thing,
Which sets my brother's slayer by my side,
Not at my feet, but honoured as a guest,
Brings not less strange a fellow with it. This,
Our enemy, comes from our enemy,   260
King Mark of Cornwall, he that harried us,
And now, being other minded, offers peace.

KING OF IRELAND.
I am well content to hold him for ally.

QUEEN.   More than ally.
He would become our kinsman, and desires   265
To bind us to his person, and has sent
His kinsman here to speak for him and ask
The hand of Iseult. Will you answer him?

KING OF IRELAND.
The hand of Iseult?

TRISTAN.   Even no less, my lord.
He is a king, but he is an old man,   270
And cannot go about the world and woo
A woman to his side. He sent me here
(Being so dear to him that he willed me King
After him, but I would have none of it)
To beg for him what, if he do not win,   275
He will not wed.

KING OF IRELAND.
               Is he so sure as that?

TRISTAN.
So sure that he has said before his lords:
"I swear that if I may not have his woman
I will have none."

KING OF IRELAND.
               That is well spoken of him.

TRISTAN.
He said, moreover, in my private ear: 280
"Say nothing of me, Tristan, but the truth:
How old I am, how grave, not easily moved,
But being moved, unalterable; a man
Not without pity, yet most just; no youth
To flatter a woman in a ballad rhyme,   285
Like you speak in stanza. Tell her this
And more," he said; "the truth: yet, win her Tristan!"

KING OF IRELAND.
Spoken like a lover rather than a king.
He could not ask for more, a mighty king,
And would not ask for less. What have you said,   290
My daughter?

ISEULT OF IRELAND.
     Nothing, I? Nothing at all.

QUEEN.
She will not answer no. Trust me, my lord.
And trouble not the girl.

ISEULT OF IRELAND.   Spoken like a king
Rather than like a lover. He who speaks them
Speaks the words well.

ISEULT OF BRITTANY.
       You are to be a queen;   295
You will be happy, Iseult.

QUEEN.   It remains
For us, my lord, to reason out this thing
And, if our kingdom claims, not to deny.
Were it not well to fetter Mark to us
With this unbreakable and silken chain?   300
What says my lord?

KING OF IRELAND. I say that it were well,
A happy thing for Ireland and for Cornwall,
And the beginning of some peace in the world.
TRISTAN.
Long live the Queen of Cornwall!
  [*All crowd up.* ISEULT OF IRELAND *turns to* BRANGAENE.]

ISEULT OF IRELAND.   Come with me,
Brangaene. We will talk of being queens;   305
Not in this market, where they bid for us,
But somewhere out of doors: I am faint for air.   307
  [*They move across the stage towards the door as the curtain falls.*]

ACT II.

The scene represents the deck of TRISTAN's *ship, partly curtained off. There is a couch against the bulwark; beside it a table, on which stands a cup.*

ISEULT OF IRELAND, *walking to and fro restlessly.*
Day and night, day and night, how many hours?

BRANGAENE.
We are two nights from Ireland, this third day
Brings us, about the second from noon,
To Cornwall.

ISEULT OF IRELAND.
        To my prison.

BRANGAENE.   To your throne.

ISEULT OF IRELAND, *pausing and speaking earnestly.*
Brangaene, I am sold to be a queen,   5
My mother sold me, Tristan bought me, Mark
Pays down the price and takes me. I have wept
Tears that the sea could never salt, such tears
The whole sea shall not wipe out of my debt.

BRANGAENE.
O mistress, you have not the eyes for tears.   10
Comfort yourself: you shall take joy to Cornwall.

ISEULT OF IRELAND.
There is none here.

BRANGAENE.   It is written in my heart.

ISEULT OF IRELAND.
It is because you love me that you say
Comfortable things to me?

BRANGAENE   The love I have
Runs forward. I am your watchdog, and I hear   15
A footstep in the dark.

ISEULT OF IRELAND.   What do your hear?
What can you hear but the old feeble feet
Of a grey king?

BRANGAENE.   Is it a little thing,
Kings will kneel down to you?

ISEULT OF IRELAND.   What do I want with knees,
That kneel because their joints are growing out?   20
I am to be an honourable wife
To the old king who harried us till age
Quieted him into fear. He would have peace,
And I am the peace-offering.

BRANGAENE.   It may be
That you will bring some peace upon yourself.   25

ISEULT OF IRELAND.
Death would bring peace: if this bright sea would lift
And take me down where Tristan could not dive
Nor Mark cast nets upon me! no, nor Iseult,
My cousin of Brittany, with her patient eyes
Weep as she did for Tristan, not for me: 30
All are against me.

BRANGAENE.   Do not think these things.
It may be joy will come to you, if not peace.

ISEULT OF IRELAND.

No, for I think too much, and there's too little
That I can do. Why is it I can do nothing?
The man I would have killed holds both my hands.   35

> [MERIADOC *comes forward, kneels, and kisses the hem of*
> ISEULT's *robe, looking up at her intently.*]

Cousin, you have some message in your eyes.
Tell it.

MERIADOC.

Iseult, I kneel to you. Iseult,
It might be now, if you will give the word.
He is unarmed, he leans beside the helm,
My men are all about him; one of them   40
Will strike the helmsman, set the helm about.
Tristan is mine: this dagger is for him.
One word, Iseult, and you are free, O queen!

TRISTAN.

Tristan is mine: why do you call him yours?
Do I note hate him worse than you do,   45
Because I am a woman? If, some day,
He break the faith that we have sworn to him,
He is yours; do with him what you will. But now
There is a bond between us, and he must live
So long as he keeps faith with his own word.   50

> [MERIADOC *rises sullenly.*]

MERIADOC.

The blood of Morolt sinks into my soul:
I have not sworn, take off your hand from me.
If it for you I wait and no not strike.
Say now that I may free my soul and yours!

ISEULT OF IRELAND.
Meriadoc, stand here. No, closer: here.   55
Give me your dagger. (*He gives her the dagger eagerly.*)
                           Do you still obey
My will because it is my will?

MERIADOC, *excitedly.*   Yes, yes!
Iseult, the word now!

ISEULT OF IRELAND, *holding out the dagger.*
                  Swear, then, on the cross
To keep your faith with Tristan while he keeps
His faith with me!

MERIADOC.   I am your slave; yet ask   60
Some other things than this.

ISEULT OF IRELAND.   Swear on this cross!

MERIADOC.
Iseult, my life is yours.

ISEULT OF IRELAND.
              Swear!

MERIADOC   Take my life
And give me this man's!

ISEULT OF IRELAND.   Swear upon the cross!

MERIADOC.
I swear.
    [*He holds out his hand over the hilt of the dagger, then takes the
    dagger and puts it back in its sheath.*]

ISEULT OF IRELAND.
    Call Tristan. I would speak with him.
    [MERIADOC *bends low and goes out.*]

BRANGAENE.
Is it well?

ISEULT OF IRELAND.
   It is well. I am tired of silence.   65
Have no fear. I will talk with him alone.
And you, for you are tired, give your eyes a rest
And go and sleep a little. I will call
If I should need you.

BRANGAENE. I am indeed sick
For lack of sleep, but should I leave you?

ISEULT OF IRELAND.   Go.   70
Sleep, rest, and come again.
   [BRANGAENE *goes out.* ISEULT *sits in meditation. There is a*
   pause, and TRISTAN *enters.*]

TRISTAN.   You sent for me.

ISEULT OF IRELAND. How is this, sir?
You did not fear, I think, to come uncalled
To Ireland.

TRISTAN. I was sent.

ISEULT OF IRELAND. You did not come
For any will of yours—that I know well;   75
And yet you come. It is not what we would,
But what we must do, that we do.

TRISTAN.   True, madam.
For me, I have always done what the sea would:
One the sea took me to you, and now again
It casts me back to you the second time.   80
I do not know why I am on this ship.

ISEULT OF IRELAND.
You are my jailer.

TRISTAN.   You are bitter, madam.

ISEULT OF IRELAND.
You have been bitter to me from the first.
Before I knew you I had never known
Sorrow; it was your courage and your craft   85
That brought sorrow upon me. What ill star
Led you from Cornwall into Ireland?

TRISTAN.   What
May not the blind stars do with us who are blind?

ISEULT OF IRELAND.
Once had your sword not eyes? But none of that.
I will but ask you why you drag me out   90
From my own land into this foreign land
To be a stranger among strangers. Where
You carry me I know not, not what price
Was paid for me, not what shall be the end.

TRISTAN.
Say what you will, I have not done you wrong   95
To bring you to a kingdom. You shall find
Peace in it and a crown; you shall have riches
And pleasure and content and idleness,
And you shall be the wife of a great king.

ISEULT OF IRELAND.
Sir, I would rather have a lower lot   100
In my own land, and love with it, than here
A loveless trouble with great riches.

TRISTAN.   No,
Not a loveless and not troubled, but the pride
And wage of beauty: all men's eyes and one
Man's love upon you.

ISEULT OF IRELAND.
                Have you such a wage?   105
Is it for love that you would have me wed
An old king in an island of my foes?

TRISTAN.
For love of love, for love of power, for pride.

ISEULT OF IRELAND.
Who shall I have to look into my eyes
That I may be his life and death to him?   110

TRISTAN.
I may not answer you. You gave me life.

ISEULT OF IRELAND.
You have been evil to me, and not good,
And yet I gave you life. Is this well done?

TRISTAN.
You gave me life. I thanked you for the gift.

ISEULT OF IRELAND.
I would have given you death. The second time   115
Why was it that I did not give your death?
Why did I give you life?

TRISTAN, *half drawing his sword ad holding the hilt toward her.*
              I give you back
The gift you gave, if you will have it back.

ISEULT OF IRELAND.
Tristan, stand fast, and keep me to my word.
I keep you to your word to me. Stand fast.   120
For there is blood between us.
     [*She starts to her feet.*]

TRISTAN.   For that blood
Have I not made advancement? Let there be
Peace between you and me.

ISEULT OF IRELAND.   What peace? What peace?

TRISTAN.
If there is no peace left us possible
There is no less one thing between us two—   125
Honour: let everything but honour die.
The past is dead already; for the future
We'll also say Amen; for what now is,
The present of this instant, I have sworn
To bring you of all women for a wife   130
Home to my lord the King. I serve my King
In all things honourable; I will serve
My Queen in all things as I serve my King.

ISEULT OF IRELAND.
Where is it written that I shall be served
By this wise enemy, who stole the peace   135
As a thief takes a jewel? If there be
Atonement for the blood that you have shed,
How can there be atonement for my peace?

TRISTAN.
All things may be forgotten.

ISEULT OF IRELAND.   All things past
Were well forgotten, when to think of them   140
Burns like a fire. Then, I should forget

That all things are forgotten, let us seal
This covenant. I will bid Brangaene—no,
Brangaene is asleep. Where is the child
Who loves to wait upon me? Child!
>   [A CHILD *puts aside the curtain and runs up.*]
>   Bring me some wine,   145
A flagon, and a cup and fill the cup.
>   [*The* CHILD *runs back and returns with a flagon and a cup,*
>   *which she fills.* ISEULT *takes it from her, and she goes quietly*
>   *back through the curtain with the empty flagon.*]
This wine shall wash out Morolt's blood. I drink
Forgetfulness, I put away my hate,
I will love no man. I will be friends with you,
Tristan, for Mark's sake, I will be a queen,   150
I will wed Mark. Pledge me! my husband, Mark!
>   [*She drinks and hands him the cup.*]

TRISTAN.
Health to Iseult, honour and peace to Mark!
>   [*He drinks. There is a long pause, and they slowly recoil from*
>   *each other, looking with amazement in each other's eyes. The cup*
>   *drops from his hands.*]

ISEULT OF IRELAND.
Tristan!

TRISTAN.
>   Iseult! O, is it life or death,
Iseult? Am I awakening into death?

ISEULT OF IRELAND.
I too, I think I am awakening.   155
Wait for me, Tristan, I have been asleep.

TRISTAN.
Iseult!

ISEULT OF IRELAND.

> I will not go to sleep again,
> But you did well to waken me. I thank you.

TRISTAN.

But yesterday death was not; nay, no more
That even such an instant point of time. 160
And there is something born into the world:
Is it death, is it love? I cannot tell;
Only it is an ending and a birth.

ISEULT OF IRELAND.

You have been crying to me in my dreams;
I heard your voice, I thought it was the sea, 165
And that awoke me, and I find you here.

TRISTAN.

I think I have been always at your side.

ISEULT OF IRELAND.

No, no, not always: I remember now,
There was another time before this time.
This is the sea, Ireland is far away; 170
But you are with me and I am awake at last.

TRISTAN.

I do not think that I am yet awake.
What is it that has bound me with these chains
That burn like shining fire about my soul?

ISEULT OF IRELAND.

What is it that has set me free? I feel 175
As if a boundless joy had given me wings:
I am as universal as the sun.
Look, Tristan. there is nothing here but light:
Light in the sky, light in the hollow sea,
The encircling and caressing light of the air! 180

Light eats into my flesh and drinks me up:
I am a cup for the immense thirst of light;
I cannot see you, Tristan, for the light.

TRISTAN.
Iseult, I see you wrapped about with light
As in a glory, clothed and garlanded.   185
And your face shines, it dazzles me; your eyes
Are burning out of brightness like two flames.

ISEULT OF IRELAND.
Tristan, I love you.

TRISTAN.   Iseult.
    [*They rush into each other's arms.*]
                        I have loved
Your hatred, now I love you for your love.

ISEULT OF IRELAND, *looking up at him, in the embrace.*
Have we been foes? I think we have been foes.   190
Look deeper, Tristan, deeper in my heart.

TRISTAN.
I look into your eyes, you have grey eyes,
They are as deep and changing as the sea,
There is not any shadow in your eyes.

ISEULT OF IRELAND, *withdrawing from the embrace.*
There is a weary, salt, and bitter thing   195
That eats my heart. I know not what it is.
    [*She moves a few steps away.*]

TRISTAN.
Yet love is stronger than the sea or death.

ISEULT OF IRELAND, *crouching down on the seat by the bulwarks.*
O what is love, and why is love so bitter
After the blinding sweetness of a moment?
I am afraid, I am afraid of love.   200
This is some death that has got hold on me;
The night is coming back into my soul.
Tristan, I am afraid. Is this is love,
I am afraid of the intolerable love.

> [*She covers her face with her hands. There is a long pause.*
> TRISTAN *looks at her in silence, then goes up to her slowly and
> touches her on the shoulder.*

TRISTAN.
Fear not, Iseult; this thing must be endured;   205
We have not sought it, it must be endured.

ISEULT OF IRELAND, *looking up slowly.*
O is this love, and must we endure love?
I did not know that love was so like death.
O sorrowful, unkind, unhappy love!

TRISTAN.
I think that from this moment we have done   210
With being happy or unhappy: all
We have to do is only to rejoice
Because we are together and alive.

ISEULT OF IRELAND.
You do not fear? You do not wonder now?
Love me no better than I love you, Tristan!   215
Tristan, I still wonder and am afraid.

TRISTAN.
Love casts out a fear, not wonder. Is it not
A thing past wonder that, of all the dust
Time shakes out of hourglass, he has made
This little hour for us to meet in?

ISEULT OF IRELAND.   Yes,   220
I will believe it, but not wonder at it.
Tristan, I am content. I will not fear.
There shall be now for us nothing of all
That has been all things to us; we are gone
A great way out into an unknown sea;   225
There is no land behind us. Look, Tristan,
The sea is naked as the hand of a man,
The sea gathers us up into its hand.
Take me in your arms and kiss me on the mouth.
    [*He takes her in his arms and kisses her.*]

BRANGAENE, *rushing in*.
O woe! O woe! O most unhappy woman!   230
What have I done? I would that I had died!
Why did you let me sleep away your life?

ISEULT OF IRELAND.
What does this mean, Brangaene?

BRANGAENE.   The cup! The cup!
    [*She snatches up the flagon from the table.*]

TRISTAN.
What of the cup?

BRANGAENE.   O mistress, there is death,
And worse than death, hid in the cup.   235

ISEULT OF IRELAND.
Why, what is worse than death?

BRANGAENE.   Love.

ISEULT OF IRELAND, *eagerly*.   And the cup,
It was the cup of love?

BRANGAENE.   It was the cup
Of love. Your mother bade me give it you
Upon your marriage-night. It would have bound
Your heart ad the King's heart, into one heart.   240
But now, but now, mistress, what have you done?

ISEULT OF IRELAND.
I have done that which shall not be undone.
Give me the cup.
>   [BRANGAENE *gives it to her reluctantly. She takes it in both*
>   *hands and holds it against her breast, reverently.*]
                    O sacred cup of love
And death, I hold you.
>   [*Then she casts it far out into the sea.*]
                         And I cast you out,
That no man save this man may drink of you,   245
Nor any other woman.

TRISTAN.   I have drunk
A poison that no man has ever tasted,
For it has withered honour in my heart
And filled my soul up with forgetfulness.
There was a king for whom I would have died.   250

ISEULT OF IRELAND.
All this shall be forgotten. What must be
Must be, and it is we who have been bound
Together, and this king I am to marry
Is as a stranger I shall never know.
Blessed by the cup of love, and, O Brangaene,   255
I bless those little hands that gave it me,
Innocent hands, not knowing what they gave.
You should also be blessed, because you slept
And all your wisdom could not hold me back
From what I had to do.

TRISTAN.   What does she say   260
Of death?

ISEULT OF IRELAND.
          Good tidings, Tristan.

BRANGAENE.   Evil tidings.
There were both love and death hid in the cup;
This cup shall be one death to both of you.

TRISTAN.
I could not love you, Iseult, and not die.
          [MERIADOC *comes in, looking scrutinizingly at the three, and
          comes forward anxiously.*]

MERIADOC.
My lady has no further use of me.   265
Now it is Tristan who must keep his faith,
And I with Tristan, for her eyes are changed.
They tell me, Tristan, that from this day forth
I have to serve you.

TRISTAN, *holding out his hand.*
                    As a friend a friend.
          [MERIADOC *clasps hands with* TRISTAN, *who moves aside and
          leans against the bulwark of the ship.*]

ISEULT OF IRELAND.
Call me the little maid.
          [MERIADOC *goes out and, after a moment, the* CHILD *enters.*]
                    Come, little one.   270
Child, give me both your hands; close to me.
I want to look at you and hold your hands.
I think I love you. Do you love me, child?

CHILD.
Yes, lady, dearly.

ISEULT OF IRELAND.
              When you brought me wine
You gave me something that you did not know,   275
And I too, did not know. I took the cup
Out of these little hands, and now I kiss
Your hands because you gave me a great gift.
      [*She kisses her two hands, one after the other.*]

CHILD.
O lady, I would give you all the world.

ISEULT OF IRELAND.
Why so you have; you have given me all the world.   280

CHILD.
I gave you nothing. When you are a queen—

ISEULT OF IRELAND.
What shall I give you when I am a queen?

CHILD.
I want to see you with a golden crown.

ISEULT OF IRELAND.
And that is all?

CHILD.   I want you to be just
As happy always as you are to-day.   285
Is it because of the crown? You used to be
Prouder, but not so happy.

ISEULT OF IRELAND.   I do not know.
Perhaps it is not good to be a queen.
I am going to a land I do not know.

CHILD, *looking away.*

Look, look, there is the land! O, is it Cornwall?   290
> [*The* CHILD *runs away and looks over the side of the ship.*
> TRISTAN *comes back towards* ISEULT *and* BRANGAENE.
> SAILORS, *etc., come forward over the deck, making preparations*
> *for landing.*]

CRIES, *within.*

Ho! Cornwall!

BRANGAENE.   Mistress!

TRISTAN.   Iseult!

CRIES, *within.*   Cornwall! Cornwall!

ISEULT OF IRELAND.

Is this my kingdom? Why, an angry shore.

Tristan, your hand, to lead my to the King!   293
> [*Smiling, she holds out her hands to him as the curtain falls.*]

ACT III.

The scene represents a garden in the palace of KING MARK *at Tintagel, over-*
looking the sea. The sea is seen below, through the trees at the edge of the rock
cliff. It is nearly dawn on a day in summer. KING MARK *comes out hurriedly*
from under the trees on the right, dragging after him MELOT *the jester, who throws*
himself at his feet.

KING MARK.
You saw the Queen?

MELOT.   My lord, I saw the Queen.
Master! forgive me!

KING MARK.   Once you saw the Queen
Under the willow-tree beside the spring;
You put a poison into both my ears:
Where was truth then?

MELOT.   Master, this tale is true.   5
It is my sorrow that I tell your truth,
Because I love you. Let the fool speak truth!

KING MARK.
I wrong no woman and no man again
For any idle speech. You have been warned.
Now, still you saw the Queen?

MELOT.   I saw the Queen,   10
Past midnight—

KING MARK.   How? You do not sleep by night?
You spy for me by night?

MELOT.   I had slept. I dreamed.

KING MARK.
Well, and your dream?

MELOT.   The horn of the white moon
Pointed.

KING MARK.
        Well, well?

MELOT.   I heard an owlet hoot
Three times; three callings.

KING MARK.   But the dream?

MELOT.   I rose.   15
Because the moon called and the owlet called;
I looked out of my window: all the ground
Was moist because of the long evening rain.
I saw his footprints.

KING MARK.   Wherefore his?

MELOT.   They led
From under Tristan's window. This truth,   20
Master, the truth of God!

KING MARK.   You followed them?

MELOT.
I followed, and where he had set his feet
I set my feet, footprint for footprint. So,
Stepping without a trace, delicately,
I came to the Queen's window.

KING MARK.   He was there?   25

MELOT.
He stood and reached his hands to her, who stood
Higher than she could reach him, though she leaned
Her right arm from the casement, murmuring.

KING MARK.
What did she say?
    [KING MARK *clutches his arm.*]
                 Come, you must say the words,
But quietly.

MELOT.   Master, you hurt me.

KING MARK.   Come,   30
The words she said.

MELOT.   I could not hear the words.
But Tristan stood and lifted up his hands,
Entreating something, and she laughed.

KING MARK.   She laughed.
Then she was only merry; a wild jest.
No more than that. And she was flushed?

MELOT.   No, pale.   35
And Tristan paler, and both as if some hunger
Starved both their faces thin.

KING MARK.   That's not so good.
And then?

MELOT   Then Tristan turned, and I drew back.
I looked again, he seemed to say farewell,
And I went softly backward in his steps,   40
Crept in at my own window, watched, and saw
Tristan returning.

KING MARK.   If this thing be true,
Which cannot be, or there's an end of truth,
Yet may be true, and then, why, Tristan's dead.
Not a word more, Melot; he was my sword: 45
Swords may dig graves; but yet it is not true.
Her eyes are naked to me, clean as light,
It is impossible to doubt her eyes.
          [*He walks away and comes back as he speaks.*]
No, no. I'll not believe it: if it be,
These two have done dishonour on their souls   50
Deep as my hurt, deeper than any hurt.
Melot, my friend, my fool, what have I done
That I should house this grief? If this be so,
My fool must pity me.
          [MELOT *embraces his feet.*]
                              I wrong myself
Even to doubt. I should not hear your words.   55

MELOT.
Have you not seen their faces as they burned
Like flame on flame?

KING MARK.   I have seen their faces burn
Like flame on flame. Why should a natural fire
Not burn? And why should we put out the day?

MELOT.
Master, master, I have not told you all.   60

KING MARK.
The truth, Melot, and, before God, the truth!

MELOT.
What if I tell you of the very hour—
It is an hour from now—here, in this garden.
Do you not hunt to-night?

KING MARK.   Before the dawn.

MELOT.
Is Tristan with you?

KING MARK.   Tristan would not come.   65

MELOT.
Before the dawn, they will be here together.
Will you be led by Melot? Go your way,
Feign to lead off the hunt; but come again,
Suddenly, in an hour, where Melot is,
And you shall take them in each other's arms.   70

KING MARK.
What if I thrust this sword into your heart
You would have me lift on Tristan?

MELOT.   Sire, to-morrow
Thrust your sword deeper down into my heart
Than any lie you find there.

KING MARK.   Who of us,
I wonder, Melot, is to die to-night?   75
I have trusted only one man in the world
And loved only one woman. If these two
Are now in league against me, I am cast out
Of unnatural and foolish heaven
They lured me into. Were it not but just   80
If with one sword I slew these two? And then—

MELOT.
My lord, my lord, you will not lift your hand
Against your own life? Swear it on the cross!
        [*He snatches up a gold cross which* KING MARK *wears on his
        chain and hold it up to him.*]

123

KING MARK.
No, no, there are no oaths for me. I speak
I know not what. Death is a woman and plays   85
A secret game with us. What shall it be
If this be true, if this impossible,
Unthinkable, all too likely thing be true?

> [*He goes slowly out, followed by* MELOT. *There is a pause, and*
> TRISTAN *and* ISEULT OF IRELAND *come slowly out from under*
> *the trees on the left. They move partly across the garden, then*
> *stop, and stand face to face.*]

ISEULT OF IRELAND.
If death should come upon us in this hour,
What would you say? Would you thank God for life?   90

TRISTAN.
                              I would thank God for life,
For I have lived, this hour, two lives in one.
Have I not held your body with my hands?
Have I not drunk your soul up with my lips?
Have I not hated you with all my love?   95

ISEULT OF IRELAND.
It is the dawn? Look up. Do not the stars
Doubt and not know if it is day or night?
Night has not been, and this is not the dawn.

TRISTAN.
It is the dawn. Why is it I must go?

ISEULT OF IRELAND.
I cannot let you go. Listen: the leaves   100
Are still, and the sea scarcely shivers. Come,
I will not let you go.

TRISTAN.   Shall I stay here
Until you bid me go?

ISEULT OF IRELAND, *gathering handfuls of roses.*
                    No, no, for that
Would never be. See where the roses burn!
These roses are the prodigals of June,   105
They burn, they waste to ashes, they are a fire
Too spendthrift of the summer. Take them, Tristan.
Do you not feel the blood of the roses burn
Between my fingers into both you hands?

TRISTAN.
I have let them fall.

ISEULT OF IRELAND.
                    Let them lie there and die   110
Before they know the long rains of the year
And weeping autumn. So should all flowers die,
And we. Will you not linger if I talk
Of roses and heap up into your hands
So many that you cannot see my face?   115
        [*They sit down on a stone seat under the trees, beside the rose-*
        bushes.]
And yet: must you not go?

TRISTAN.   The light begins
To search into your eyes. Is it your face?
I shall not find it when I look again.

ISEULT OF IRELAND, *grasping her arms around him.*
I cannot let you go; I put my hand
About your neck; I hold you with my hands.   120
You will not leave me while I hold you fast?

TRISTAN.
How should I leave my love, my sustenance,
And go into exile willingly?
And yet you catch at me as if you feared
That I would let you go.

ISEULT OF IRELAND   I hold you fast   125
Because I fear: hold me and comfort me.
Swear over the old oaths, they are all here,
Here is my scarf; but sweat them over, Tristan,
Before you go, and kiss me in the neck.

TRISTAN.
I have no words that can be said twice over.   130
     [*He kisses her.*]

ISEULT OF IRELAND.
Tristan, it is my life
Your lips drink up: I cannot bear your lips:
I feel them to the marrow of my bones.
O I would be a fire and burn your lips,
O I would be a beast and eat your lips,   135
I would annihilate their sweetness. Now
My blood is all an anguish of desire.
Speak, slay me, do not kiss me. Kiss me now!

TRISTAN, *drawing back from her and looking to her eyes.*
Iseult, there is an end,
Men say, to love.

ISEULT OF IRELAND.
                    O foolish men!

TRISTAN.   For us   140
Shall our love have an end? Shall time pluck out
Our eyes, put out our blood? Shall we two see
Each other and not tremble? I hold your hands
In both my hands: one day shall we take hands
And not a vein in either of them leap up   145
To bid the other welcome?

ISEULT OF IRELAND.   What shall time
Steal from the blood? What is there he can steal
Out of the marrow that is in the bones?

TRISTAN.
Nothing; that blood and marrow, these remain,
But there is something over in the soul   150
That will not be cast out. I have drunk up
All but forgetfulness.

ISEULT OF IRELAND.
                        I have drunk up
Forgetfulness. It was a bitter draught;
Lees of the drink: Mark and a marriage-bed!
But the first draught, the sweetness of it, Tristan!   155

TRISTAN.
I have forgotten that I had a friend.
He would have thrust a crown upon me, but
I had no uses for it. No man lived
Another as he loved me, and now, now
My neck is set into a felon's noose: 160
I am dragged up and down here in the dust.

ISEULT OF IRELAND.
Love is a sword, and the sword severs friends;
Love is a fire and burns all lesser things.
Love is not love
Unless it root up honour like a weed.   165

TRISTAN.
Love is not love unless it honour
Above all mortal beings.

ISEULT OF IRELAND.   There is a thing
Which is the faith of love: I know none else,
No other God, or king, or counsellor,
No crown, no joy, no glory, and it devours   170
All pleasures and all bonds and is flame
No wind shall put out.

TRISTAN.　　　　　Only now a wind
Has put my honour out, as a wind blows
A candle out, and all the room is dark.

ISEULT OF IRELAND.
Why will you cry that barren bastard word　　　　175
Honour? I tell you, Tristan, I would now
Walk up the minster aisle at Caerleon,
Barefoot before the bishops and their God,
And hold the red-hot iron in my hand.
Fire would not burn me: God would do me right:　　180
I have not sinned against the honour of love.

TRISTAN.
What I have done that any woman born
Should love me so beyond her soul? God knows
That I must have you, Iseult, beyond death.
　　　[*He kneels down and kisses her hand.*]

ISEULT OF IRELAND.
Death shall end all things: we are quiet then:　　　185
I shall not want you love when I am dead:
Take back your honour and let it warm your grave;
But, till the grasses creep and cover me,
Tristan, this is my body and my blood,
And they are yours.

TRISTAN.　　　　　The world passes away,　　　190
You have put the world into a dusty pit,
And all is covered up. Do with my life
What you would do with it.

ISEULT OF IRELAND.　　　Shall I know you soul?
Tristan, what if the King should find us here?

TRISTAN.
I would not raise my hand against my King:　　　195
If he would slay me, he has but to strike.

ISEULT OF IRELAND, *starting to her feet.*
Coward to me!
Let Mark's right hand fumble about your heart
With the hunting knife that never killed a deer!
Have I no place there? Would you have him find me   200
There, where he looks to find me?

TRISTAN.   He is my King.

ISEULT OF IRELAND.
Will you be false to me, and for a king?

TRISTAN.
Why do you look upon me with such eyes?

ISEULT OF IRELAND.
Tristan, take hold of me, and hold me fast,
And hurt my fingers between both your hands,   205
And kiss me on the lips, and say I have lied!

TRISTAN.
I kiss you head that God made for a crown,
But I will swear no oaths now any more:
We have said all that need be said till death.

ISEULT OF IRELAND.
Now, go; go quickly; for the dawn is here.   210
How soon it comes! I did not see it come,
And how the day has all its eyes on us.
Hark, what was that? No, do not stir.
        [*She seizes him.*]
TRISTAN.   I hear
Brangaene calling.

ISEULT OF IRELAND.
                    She is running, see.
Under the trees.
        [BRANGAENE *comes towards them, running.*

129

BRANGAENE.   Mistress!

ISEULT OF IRELAND.

                      Why do we know   215
The thing before it comes and not believe it?
Is it the King, Brangaene?

BRANGAENE.   It is the King!

ISEULT OF IRELAND.
Were we not talking, Tristan, of to-morrow?
There shall be no tomorrow. This is well.

BRANGAENE, *panting*.
The King came to the gate, he stayed at the gate;   220
Melot rose up out of a spying corner
And whispered in his ear; Melot had seen
Lord Tristan when he entered; the King turned;
Melot and he went stealthily away;
Melot turned back and watched at the gate;   225
But now is the King gone to summon these
That shall be eyes to him and see his shame.

ISEULT OF IRELAND.
Tristan, there is no need now any more
To make a hooded secret of our love;
Soon the whole world shall look into our hearts   230
Because Mark wills it. The King's will be done.

TRISTAN.
I have undone the glory of your crown:
Men shall speak evil of you for my sake:
I would that Mark had stabbed me in my sleep!

ISEULT OF IRELAND.
Now I am glad, utterly glad at last,   235
This first time wholly since the day of days
We drank down love together. I have my will,

I have always willed that he should take us thus.
    [*She takes* TRISTAN's *hand*.]
Is he not long in coming? Go, Brangaene,
Open the door for the King's coming' bring   240
My lord the King and greet him from his wife.

    [KING MARK *enters, closely followed by* MELOT; *behind them
the lords of the court, in hunting dress.* KING MARK *pauses and
the comes slowly forward.*]

KING MARK, *to* ISEULT.
Queen, I have come to take you to your throne.
My kingdom cannot spare you; you are wise,
Wiser than women: I have need of you.
There has been also some particular love   245
By which, in the past, I have been bound to you:
That will I lay aside, needing it not.
These lords bear witness you are my true Queen;
You have been dear to me, being my wife,
And I have something that I will not say;   250
Only, I do you honour as my Queen.
    [KING MARK *turns slowly to* TRISTAN.]
But you, blood of my blood, sword of my sword,
I have no words to be avenged on you.
I shall wipe Cornwall clean of such a shame.
This, my good lords, is Tristan, my sister's son,   255
My son, if he had willed to be my son;
I would have given him up my kingdom: he,
For honour's sake and for your sake, my lords,
Would none of it; he would not take my crown.
O baser, infinite ingratitude,   260
He would not take my kingdom; no, he would
That I should wed him from inheritance.
He brought me this—this Queen to be my wife,
That he might take a woman from my bed.
O Tristan, there are many souls in hell   265
That have not dragged so base as this
Out of the night and judgement-place of God.

TRISTAN, *who was drawn back, with bowed head.*
King! Master!

KING MARK.
          He is speechless.

ISEULT OF IRELAND.   Let me speak!
Only, my lord, bid these gone from us:
We have no need of any witness now.   270
     [KING MARK *motions to the* LORDS, *who go out.*]

MELOT, *as he goes.*
I have cracked the nut; they will scramble for the pieces.
     [*He goes out.*]

KING MARK.
Iseult, is there, then, anything to say?

ISEULT OF IRELAND.
My lord, you see that Tristan cannot speak,
You see that Tristan is too honourable
To speak the truth. I am a woman, sir.   275
And women have no honour mixed in the blood
That sways a man for loving. You and I
Were set into one bed because two lands
Had torn too long at one another's throats:
I brought you Ireland, and you gave me Cornwall.   280
What did you give me in a little earth
That weighs no more than mine? I am alive
Wherever there is the earth under me.
There is living not meshed into your crown,
There is a thing, my Lord, most necessary   285
To every soul that comes into the world:
I have not stolen it, Tristan gave it me.
He did not rob you: he had it of himself,
You cannot punish us because we loved.

KING MARK.
I loved you; you have wronged me in my love.   290

ISEULT OF IRELAND.
This love is innocent as life or death.
The open unastonished eyes of day
Look on it and are not ashamed. There is
No other living thing necessary in the world.
But you have killed it, and for your own sake   295
Dragged your own honour in the dust. Now, now,
What will you do for love's sake?

KING MARK, *turning from her.*   Tristan first.
Stand up before me, Tristan. Answer me:
Will your tongue speak this woman's evil words?
No, you are silent; there is still a little,   300
A little honour left. You turn from her:
Your forehead is penitent for shame.

TRISTAN.
I turn to you, my King, but not from her;
For I have wronged you. If I have brought wrong
Upon the Queen of Cornwall, not my life   305
Shall ransom my misdeed; for what besides
Now lies between us, there is nothing left
For me to do, nothing to undo; all
Is over, and the end of things has come.
If there is any honour left in me,   310
It may be honour shall yet make me whole.

KING MARK.
Tristan, give me your sword.
        [TRISTAN *gives him his sword, which he breaks across his knee
        and throws on the ground.*
                        Your sword I break,
Only I leave you, not for pity, life.
It may be you will yet redeem your honour;

133

But here, no more; you are as one now dead,   315
Cast out of the clean honest midst of us.
I banish you from Cornwall.
> [ISEULT OF IRELAND *springs forward and draws out a naked*
> *dagger, which she offers to* TRISTAN.]

ISEULT OF IRELAND.   No, not that!
Kill Mark!

TRISTAN, *putting by her hand gently.*
I have been conquered, and all's vain, Iseult.
If you have loved me, be a little sorry   320
And you, my King, forgive me.
> [*He goes out slowly and with bent head.*]

KING MARK.   Iseult, come!   321
> [*He holds out his hand to her as the curtain falls.*]

ACT IV.

The scene represents a room in the castle in Brittany; at the back is window over-looking the sea. On the left TRISTAN *lies in bed, asleep. By the side of the bed is a table, on which stands a flagon of wine and a cup. There is a door on the right.* ISEULT OF BRITTANY *is watching beside* TRISTAN. ELAINE *stands at the foot of the bed.*

ISEULT OF BRITTANY.
Look out and see if you can see the ship.

ELAINE.
Madam, there is not a sail upon the sea.

ISEULT OF BRITTANY.
Is the wind rising?

ELAINE.   The wind is striking
The waves like a great hammer on the walls.

ISEULT OF BRITTANY, *bending over* TRISTAN *and then moving away.*
He is asleep. Call the physician in.   5

    [ELAINE *goes to door and beckons. The* PHYSICIAN *comes in.*]

PHYSICIAN.
Madam, must I speak comfortable words
Or speak the truth?

ISEULT OF BRITTANY.
                The truth.

PHYSICIAN.   All things are possible
To our divine and undivulged art:
It may be he will live.

ISEULT OF BRITTANY.
                              It may be? Speak
More comfortable words, and yet speak truth.   10

PHYSICIAN.
All things being possible in medicine,
And all things known that may destroy or heal
Being known to the great doctor of Salerno
We look for the ship that Tristan sent,
It may be that this lord of secret things   15
Has found some magic herb of Italy
We know not of, north of the western waters.
If he have found some curable accident
Of nature, and how poison can lick up
Poison, my lord may still be saved; and yet,   20
If he should live—

ISEULT OF BRITTANY.
                              If he should live?

PHYSICIAN.   The wonder
Will outpace memory, for so fierce a wound,
So deadly venomed, I have never seen.
The knife that pierced him was a savage knife,
Dipped in some foul, unnatural broth of death,   25
Poisoning the sources, and his blood is turned
Quite out of the honest current of the blood.

ISEULT OF BRITTANY.
It was the poisoned knife of Meriadoc.
The knife was not so mortal as it was
When Tristan struck him back.

PHYSICIAN.   He struck the heart;   30
The traitor's hand was not so sure; the wound
Had healed by now but for the poison in it.
Whence had this man so fierce a drug? The like
Is only brewed by witches over sea.

ISEULT OF BRITTANY.
A witch, yes, a most deadly Irish witch.   35

PHYSICIAN.
This poison has been bought at a great price.

ISEULT OF BRITTANY.
A great price paid in hell and hoarded up
To be my wedding gift. Must Tristan die?

PHYSICIAN.
'T is a strange thing he has lived so many days,
Outlived the limit. Something holds him still,   40
I know not what, to life. Does my lord desire
The questionable gift of life so much?
Men dying have lived on by willing it.

ISEULT OF BRITTANY.
I did not know that he loved life so much.
He has been moody, he has only cared   45
For fighting in the field, I have never seen
A joyous ardour in him since he came
Back to our coasts, not even when he drove
The enemies from our gates and gave my father
Hid dukedom back.

PHYSICIAN.   Did he not take the hand   50
Of the duke's noble daughter for a gift
And guerdon? He has reason to love life.

ISEULT OF BRITTANY.
Seek for it elsewhere.

PHYSICIAN.   It may be in the ship.
Does he not question eagerly of the ship
We wait for from Salerno?

ISEULT OF BRITTANY.   Eagerly.   55

PHYSICIAN.
Hope bids him live. He lives until he sees
The ship and then—God send him grace therewith!

ISEULT OF BRITTANY.
I thank you. You have put into my heart
A little seed of hope, and it will grow.
Go quietly. He still sleeps. He must not wake.   60
     [*The* PHYSICIAN *goes out.*]

ELAINE.
O lady, is there any hope?

ISEULT OF BRITTANY.   All hope,
This learned man has told me, all hope now
Is in the ship. My lord will surely live
Until the ship is here.

ELAINE.   And then?

ISEULT OF BRITTANY.   Why, then,
He is saved.

ELAINE.   Who is this lady that is coming   65
To save him?

ISEULT OF BRITTANY.
          Lady?

ELAINE.   Might this lady be
Some kinswoman or cousin of my lady?

ISEULT OF BRITTANY.
Why who then?

ELAINE.   She who is coming in the ship.

ISEULT OF BRITTANY.
There is no woman coming in the ship.
The ship is coming from Salerno with   70
The greatest leech in Italy.

ELAINE.   But no,
How can that be?

ISEULT OF BRITTANY.
                  Why not?

ELAINE.   Because the ship
Set sail for Cornwall.

ISEULT OF BRITTANY, *startling*.
                  Cornwall?

ELAINE.   Was it not?

ISEULT OF BRITTANY, *checking herself*.
Ah, yes, to Cornwall. How did you know, my child?

ELAINE.
I listened—

ISEULT OF BRITTANY.
            Yes.

ELAINE.   I heard, although my lord   75
Spoke low. He bade take ship—

ISEULT OF BRITTANY.   To Cornwall?

ELAINE.   Yes,
With speed, and bring back speedily—

ISEULT OF BRITTANY.   Yes, bring—

ELAINE.
The name was yours, madam, the Lady Iseult!

TRISTAN, *in his sleep, loudly.*
Iseult!

ELAINE.
        My lord is calling to you.

ISEULT OF BRITTANY.   Not to me.
He is talking in his sleep.
(*Moving towards the bed.*) Was it to me   80
Tristan, or to the one woman in the world?
(*To* ELAINE.) I will watch beside him. Let me be alone.
        [ELAINE *goes out, and* ISEULT OF BRITTANY *walks to and fro
        in dejection.*]
Iseult is coming in the ship: he lives
Until the ship is here. She will come in
And take my husband, who was never hers,   85
Out of my arms. I have not stolen her name;
It is my own poor name. I have not stolen
Her love from this proud queen: it is still hers,
He is all hers, but he is also mine.
Why should she come, being so rich to me   90
Who am so poor? Must beggars give back alms?

This man is mine, I hold him: better dead
And mine, than hers and living. What have I said?
It is this deadly woman whom I hate
That comes to bring him death. He shall not die.   95
Shall she suck out her poison in his wound?
She would not save him. Could I give him back
Into her hands if she would heal him? O
The bitterness of love, the hate of love,
So kind in the beginning and so sharp   100
A sickle when the seed has come to ear!
What am I but a woman, who loves only
The man who she has held between her arms?
Shall I begin to hate him for her sake,
Because he loved no other than this fair,   105
This deadly royal woman of my name,
The other Iseult? Me he never loved.
Would that the sea drank her, and that her ship
Were gulped down living by a wide-mouthed wave!
She shall not take him from me while she lives.   110

TRISTAN, *in sleep.*
Iseult!

ISEULT OF BRITTANY.
        He is calling on her in his sleep,

TRISTAN, *half awakening.*
Say nothing more. If I am sick to death,
There is one ending; but no tears, Iseult.
Open the window.

ISEULT OF BRITTANY, *going to the window and opening it.*
                        So?

TRISTAN.   Open it wide.
Do you not see a sail?

ISEULT OF BRITTANY.
                There is no sail.   115
The wind is cold, and there is a grey rain.
Shall I not close the window?

TRISTAN, *rising from his bed.*
                Listen! A cry.
It is the sea. Tell me, is it the sea?
There is another crying, but it is here,
Here in my wrists and forehead; but this voice   120
Is louder than the little voice of the blood.
Iseult, listen, and tell me if you hear.

ISEULT OF BRITTANY.
I hear the wind rushing and the waves beat.

TRISTAN.
Oh no, oh no.
It is the crying of an incurable wound,   125
It turns on a sick bed and cannot sleep,
It cries to me, and I am sick, I am sick.
    [*He falls back on his bed.*]

ISEULT OF BRITTANY, *coming up to the bed.*
You must be quieter than a sea-swallow
Upon a rocking wave. You know out birds
Find homes in the loud middle of the storm   130
When we are frightened. Cannot you, my lord,
Look for some piece and solace in this pain?

TRISTAN.
No, no, I can but cry as the sea cries.
I am as angry with my pain, as weak
And angry as the sea that hates the wind.   135
But you are gentle as a feathered thing
That the wind carries: and you do not fear the sea?
You do not fear me, Iseult?

ISEULT OF BRITTANY.   My dear lord,
There is some cruel stranger in your heart
I indeed fear; but you are always gentle,   140
And when you look at me and speak my name
You can say my name as if indeed you loved me.

TRISTAN.
I made a song once, all men sing it now,
The song of Iseult, Tristan's life and death,
And women weep to hear it, and men too.   145
I made it with the sorrow of the world
And with the sorrow in the hearts of men.

ISEULT OF BRITTANY.
Your eyes are full of tears to think of it.
Is it your pain? I would not, though the name
Be mine, that it should hurt you.

TRISTAN.   Love made the name.   150
It is a heart-shaped talisman and holds
The very heart of love. I say it over
Like something I remember in my sleep.

ISEULT OF BRITTANY.
I heard you say it in your sleep to-day.

TRISTAN.
Look, that was a white thing; it dipped in the wind: 155
A white bird; a good messenger. Look out,
Iseult, and tell me if you see a sail.

ISEULT OF BRITTANY, *going to the window.*
I see the grey sea and the grey sea. Nothing.

TRISTAN.
I am sick, Iseult; but if that ship would come,
It would bring life. He knows the medicine   160
That heals me even of death: he brings me life.

ISEULT OF BRITTANY.
Has this physician from Salerno, then,
So infinite a skill?

TRISTAN.   Infinite skill!

ISEULT OF BRITTANY.
Is he a man of books or does he find
Secret in herbs and healing in the earth?   165

TRISTAN.
All things are possible to love: he loves.

ISEULT OF BRITTANY.
He comes himself, if you but send for him?

TRISTAN.
I do not know if he will come himself;
But if he come, I know that I shall live.

ISEULT OF BRITTANY.
Tristan, if I had skill to bring you to life,   170
As I have will to do it and love too,
You should not need this coming; but alas,
I have but will and love and nothing else.
I cannot hear you, but if the Mother of God
Be yet in heaven the mother of us men,   175
You shall be healed.

TRISTAN.   Have you been praying, Iseult?

ISEULT OF BRITTANY.
I have not ceased to pray.

TRISTAN.   Shall God forgive?
I think that God did never yet forgive.

ISEULT OF BRITTANY.
Lie quiet in your bed and do not think
About these things that we shall never know.   180
There have been prayers that saved from death.

TRISTAN.   Not so.
I shall lay by my glory, with my soul,
And where my body, that feasted and lay warm,
Is sewn into a clout, then shall my hall
Be made with a spade, and my bower builded soon;   185
Worms shall come in to be my guests in the dark.

ISEULT OF BRITTANY.
Why do you murmur over these old words
That the priests say in Latin?

TRISTAN.   There shall be,
In his grave, no forgetting.

ISEULT OF BRITTANY.   You shall live!

TRISTAN, *starting up*.
Why do you wake me? There is a sail?

ISEULT OF BRITTANY.   No sail!   190

TRISTAN, *wildly*.
Do you not see I am dying hour by hour,
And yet you will not come!

ISEULT OF BRITTANY.   Hush, you speak wildly.
TRISTAN.
Iseult!

ISEULT OF BRITTANY.
        See, I am here.

TRISTAN.   No, no, O God!
This agony that eats into my side,
This hurrying possessing my blood,   195
This rat that gnaws me; this insatiable
And intimate infinity of pain
Will not delay: the ship, the ship delays!

ISEULT OF BRITTANY.
Lie quietly, my lord; think not of this.

TRISTAN.
Is the sail black or white? If it be black,   200
It is a shroud the colour of my hope.
The sail is white, sad that the sail is white!

ISEULT OF BRITTANY.
What should the sail betoken?

TRISTAN.   Why, my end.
It is the white wing of a the bird in the sky
I saw out there, flying against the wind.   205
Why do you ask me what the white sail means?
If it be white—

ISEULT OF BRITTANY, *eagerly*.
            If it be white?

TRISTAN, *in a low voice, sinking back*.
                I am saved.

ISEULT OF BRITTANY, *aside*.
If she is coming, it is the white sail;
But if she is not coming, the black sail.
(*To* TRISTAN.) What if it be the black sail?

TRISTAN, *faintly*.   The black sail,   210
I have forgotten what it means.

ISEULT OF BRITTANY, *moving towards the window.*
Now, now,

I am to do with this man what I will
For the first time. I hold him in both hands
Now. Am I still Iseult of the White Hands?
I have to give her signal to him, and for her   215
Tell him that she is coming. If she comes,
Who knows? It may be that the sail is black.
How can I see that sail and see it white?

TRISTAN, *feebly.*
There is no sail?

ISEULT OF BRITTANY.
There is no sail. The sea

Is empty, but the wind rises on it.   220

TRISTAN, *half unconscious.*
When we are dead—

ISEULT OF BRITTANY, *running to the bedside.*
My lord!

TRISTAN.   No, they shall sing
No evil songs of us when we are dead;
They shall sing songs of us.

ISEULT OF BRITTANY.   O!

TRISTAN.   Happy lovers,
Because we drank one love out of one cup,
And death is not so sure.

ISEULT OF BRITTANY.
O! O!

TRISTAN.   Iseult,   225
(*Looking into vacancy.*) I have been faithful, Iseult.

ISEULT OF BRITTANY, *shrinking away.*   Now he sees
The other woman, and he cries to her.

TRISTAN.
Give me the cup.
> [*She takes the cup from beside his bed and pours wine into it.*]

ISEULT OF BRITTANY.
                     Here, Tristan! Here is wine.
See, I will set my lips to it—

TRISTAN, *snatching it from her.*
                     No, no,
You must not drink it. What is in the cup?   230

ISEULT OF BRITTANY.
Wine for your thirst, Tristan.

TRISTAN.   This is no wine.
You do not know what this is. Set it down.
> [*She sets it down by the bedside. He again looks into vacancy.*]
Have you forgotten, Iseult, and so soon?
It was not wine: I will not drink it twice,
I would not forget twice. Was it the cup   235
That put the faithful unforgetting fire
Into my marrow?

ISEULT OF BRITTANY.
                     No, it was the knife:
Did you not know? the knife of Meriadoc.

TRISTAN.
The blood of Morolt cries out of the knife,
Yet this is not his vengeance: it is hers.   240
It was for her he let her mother's poison
Into my side. You loved her, Meriadoc.
Have you loved better than I have? Iseult,

Where are you gone? You were here by my bed,
You would have healed me: someone thrust you back.   245
What are these white hands that I see, there, there,
Thrusting you back until you fade away?
I cannot see you any longer. Who
Is this pale woman with the angry eyes?
(*Looking at* ISEULT.)
You are beautiful and yet I do not know you.   250
          [ISEULT *covers her face with her hands.*]

ISEULT OF BRITTANY.
I am not angry, but you kill my heart.
Do you not know me, Tristan? Look at me.

TRISTAN.
I pray you, do not weep: but if you are
As pitiful as your weeping shows you, turn
And tell me if there is a sail upon the sea.   255

ISEULT OF BRITTANY, *going back to the window.*
Tristan, there is a sail!

TRISTAN.   O do not mock me.
Is there indeed a sail?

ISEULT OF BRITTANY.
                    Yes, yes a sail.
The ship is close under the castle walls.
It comes around the corner of the rocks.
It is close now, quite close.

TRISTAN, *starting up.*   Did I not know   260
That I had but to call and she would come?

ISEULT OF BRITTANY.
He calls to her: he sees her in the ship.

Tristan.
I have been lying in my grave, I think,
These years, and she is coming to waken me.

Iseult of Brittany.
These years, these years!

Tristan.   All will be well.

Iseult of Brittany.   Already   265
He knows me with his eyes: his eyes
See her already, he smiles to welcome her.
There is a great joy in his eyes: it kills
My heart. She shall not take him from my heart.

Tristan
The sail! the sail! Look, look, can you not see   270
The colour of the sail?

Iseult of Brittany.
                    What shall I say?
Tears in my eyes blind me. I cannot see
What colour the sail is.

Tristan.   The sail is white!
Iseult of Brittany.
The wind is tossing it, and the sea leaps
After the ship. She will be in the ship.   275
O wind and sea, why were you merciful?
She will be here. He sees her. What shall I say?
I will not be her messenger to him.

Tristan.
Look straight.

Iseult of Brittany.
                    I see, I see.

TRISTAN.   Is the sail white?

ISEULT OF BRITTANY, *slowly turning her eyes at* TRISTAN.
                            The sail is black.   280

TRISTAN, *after a pause, slowly, in a feint voice, looking straight in front*
  of him with ecstatic eyes.
God bless you, Iseult; and good-night.
        [*He falls back dead.*]

ISEULT OF BRITTANY, *rushing forward and leaning over him.*
                                            Tristan,
It is a white sail. She is coming, Tristan.
Lift up your head, listen: Iseult is here!
        [*She tries to raise his head.*]
O——h! what have I done? No, no,
Wake, wake, Tristan, and let me die for you!   285
        [*She flings herself on the bed, then rises and cries.*]
Ygraine! Elaine! Imogen! He is dead.
        [*The women rush in, followed by the* PHYSICIAN.]
My lord is dead. I killed him, I myself.
Come closer. See, he is quite dead, quite dead.
You thought I loved him; but I killed him. Yet
I only spoke a word.
        [*She bursts into hysterical weeping. Her women support her.*]
YGRAINE   Lead her away.   290
This sorrow is too heavy for her.

ISEULT OF BRITTANY, *to the* PHYSICIAN.
                            Sir,
You must awaken him: he is only sleeping.
You told me he would live till the ship came.
The ship is come. Why do you look at him
As if there were now nothing more to do?   295
Can you not make him lift one of these lids
That cover his eyes down from seeing her?
For he must see her. She is at the gate.
Wake him, wake him, and I will go away.

PHYSICIAN.
Madam, I cannot wake him.

ISEULT OF BRITTANY.   But I will.   300
     [*She leans over the bed.*]
Will you not waken, and look on me once,
Tristan, before she comes?

ELAINE.   Come, lady.

IMOGEN.   Come,
You will go wild with sorrow. Come with us.

ISEULT OF BRITTANY, *listens fearfully, hearing sounds without, then
     sits down by the bedside and takes hold of* TRISTAN's *hand.*
Tristan, she is coming: do not let me go!

          [*She stares fearfully at the door, which is thrown open, and*
          ISEULT OF IRELAND *appears on the threshold.* BRANGAENE
          follows her. The women stand about the bed in which TRISTAN's
          body lies, with heads bent and drooping hands. ISEULT OF
          IRELAND *looks through them to the dead body.*]

ISEULT OF IRELAND, *on the threshold, to* BRANGAENE.
Tristan is dead, and there is nothing left   305
In all the world. I have not come too late.

ISEULT OF BRITTANY.
Too late, too late! I told him that the sail
Was black. I killed him. It was I who killed him.

ISEULT OF IRELAND.
Comfort yourself, Iseult of Brittany.
And hide your head and weep, if you will weep,   310
Because it had to be, and leave me here.
You have done nothing in this mighty death.

ISEULT OF BRITTANY.
Where shall I go? for I have killed my lord.
> [*She rises and with bowed head moves slowly away between her women, who lead out of the door.*]

ISEULT OF IRELAND, *going up to the bed.*
I kiss you for the last time on the mouth,
Tristan.
> [*She bends over and kisses him and then speaks over his body.*]
>> He was the glory of the world;   315
All the world's dust, for Tristan can be dead.
This dust was once a fire and burned the stars:
Now what a little ashes holds the fire
That was blown out too early. There is nothing
Left in the world, and I am out of place.   320
Could you not wait for me until I came,
Tristan?
> [*She lies down beside him and dies.*]

BRANGAENE.
Mistress! my life! O she is dead. O lady,
Now you have you desire and are at rest
(*To the* ATTENDANTS.) Come nearer, all of you, lay them royally
And side by side, body by body. Come.   325
Lift up her head, that his may not outtop
The fairest head in the world. You shall lie so.
Have you no rich cloths to lay over them?
Bring something to make up a royal bed.
> [*The* ATTENDANTS *bring forward rich cloths and lay over them.* BRANGAENE *arranges them with care. An* ATTENDANT *rushes in.*]

ATTENDANT.
The other ship is here. It is King Mark.   330
With all his lords.

BRANGAENE.   He is not to come in
Until this work is over. Is all ready?
> [*The door is flung open, and* KING MARK *rushes in, followed
> by the* LORDS.]

KING MARK.
Where is Iseult? Is Tristan here?

BRANGAENE, *going towards him and raising her hand to impose silence.*
                              No, King.
They are not here. Look where they are.
> [*The* ATTENDANTS *draw aside, disclosing the two bodies.*
> KING MARK *comes forward.*]

KING MARK.   Is death
Treacherous? Has he gone faster than I could?   335
Could I not come upon them in one bed
But death must find them first? I am too late.
There is no room for my revenge.

BRANGAENE, *coming forward.*   O King,
There is no room here for revenge. These two
Drank from one cup, not knowing, the long sorrow   340
Now ended in this death.
KING MARK.   The cup of love?

BRANGAENE.
It was the cup of love: the Queen of Ireland
Prepared a cup of love to bind your heart
To hers who now lies dead: she on the ship
Drank ignorantly with him who now lies dead   345
The cup of love you should have drunk with her.
There had been love between you: but these have loved
Not well or ill, but of necessity.

KING MARK.
Their love has wrought this evil of itself,
If it be evil to have died together.   350
Had I but known! Tristan, had I but know!
Had my son Tristan but had faith in me
And told me all the truth, then had I given
Iseult, whom I have loved, to be his wife.
But now has all this woe come to an end   355
In sorrow, and because we were all blind.
The woman whom I loved, and my one friend,
Lie here, and I am living still. So be it.
They shall be buried like a king and queen
Among the kings my fathers. Bear these two   360
Back to Tintagel. I will follow them.

THE END.

Lightning Source UK Ltd.
Milton Keynes UK
UKHW011129031221
395039UK00001B/129